JAIPUR
CITY PALACE

ISBN: 978-81-7436-569-9

© Giles Tillotson & Vibhuti Sachdev 2008
This edition published in arrangement with
Roli & Janssen BV, The Netherlands
M-75 Greater Kailash II (Market),
New Delhi 110 048, India
Ph: ++91-11-29212782, 29210886;
Fax: ++91-11-29217185
E-mail: roli@vsnl.com; Website: rolibooks.com

Editor: Priyanka Chowdhury & Eman Chowdhary
Design: Nitisha Mehta
Layout: Nabanita Das
Production: Naresh Nigam, Kumar Raman

Printed and bound in Singapore

JAIPUR
CITY PALACE

VIBHUTI SACHDEV & GILES TILLOTSON

Lustre Press
Roli Books

CONTENTS

INTRODUCTION:
THE HISTORY AND CULTURE OF AN INDIAN COURT

The city of Jaipur, now the capital of Rajasthan in western India, was formerly the centre of an autonomous state which flourished under Mughal and then British supremacy between the 18th and the 20th centuries. The state itself was of much earlier origin, having been created a thousand years ago by a migrating Rajput clan that seized territory from local tribes. This state was then known as Dhundhar, which remained its proper name, though it has more generally been called Amber after its capital city through most of the Mughal period. Following the transfer of the capital to a new site inaugurated in 1727, it became Jaipur.

The City Palace in Jaipur was established at the same time as the new city itself by one of the most distinguished figures in late Mughal history, Maharaja Sawai Jai Singh II (r. 1699-1743). A leading Hindu ruler of his time, he is remembered today as a statesman, an astronomer and a patron of the arts. From the date of its foundation until 1949, his palace served as the principal ceremonial residence of Sawai Jai Singh's successors and as the administrative centre of the Jaipur court. This period of over two hundred years saw the transition from one empire to another and, indeed, the eventual transfer of power to democratic rule in the region. With that last change the palace ceased to function as a seat of administration, as the state previously governed from it was absorbed, along with its neighbours, into the new Indian Union in the years that immediately followed Independence. Today the palace continues to be used in part as a residence and partly as a privately owned museum and tourist attraction.

Left: Two of the courts of the City Palace, with the clock tower and Jantar Mantar beyond

Facing page: Maharaja Sawai Jai Singh II, portrait by Sahib Ram

Page 2: Painted relief carving in the Pritam Niwas Chowk

Page 3: A mural in the Zanana Mahal

Page 4-5: Entrance to a courtyard in the Zanana Mahal

Women playing
pacchisi; Jaipur
School, 18ᵗʰ century

Preceding pages:
The palace at
Amber; photograph
by Lala Deen Dayal

The palace comprises a number of buildings spread out over an area approximately one square kilometre in extent. Though a substantial number of them date from the mid-18ᵗʰ century, others were added later at various times up until the mid-20ᵗʰ century. This history makes the Jaipur City Palace one of India's most important court complexes: it is the most extensive palace of a Hindu ruler of the Mughal era to have survived intact, while at the same time it illustrates the last two centuries of the development of Indian palace architecture at a single site.

Throughout its long history, the Jaipur City Palace was much more than the residence of a maharaja. It also served as a site of religious ritual, a place of entertainment, a centre of political administration and court ceremony, as well as a source of patronage for music, literature, dance and painting. This book is therefore not a study of architecture alone, but of the many functions that were accommodated within its walls. Accordingly, the arrangement of the chapters (outlined below) is not chronological, but thematic, as each chapter deals with one prominent aspect of court life.

The opening chapter, entitled 'The Dynastic Succession', briefly reviews the reigns of each of the ten successive maharajas who ruled from Jaipur, but focusses attention on the manner in which the throne passed from one generation to another. This process was ostensibly governed by rules but, in practice, was open to challenge and contest. Our intention here is not to revive old controversies for their own sake but to show how courtly politics were more fluid than hindsight often makes them appear. Courtly expressions of loyalty and obedience might create an impression of a general bending to the inevitable, but such an impression belies the actual state of things: a maharaja's authority had to be constantly asserted and negotiated in a process that involved a range of interested parties, both within the court and beyond. Historians tend to overlook the losers in this game in much the same spirit as they shun counter-factuals. 'What if this rival had won?' 'What if things had fallen out this other way, which at one point looked possible?' Such questions are unanswerable. But we would diminish our understanding if, while dismissing the might-have-beens, we overlook too the processes that once brought them into play. The chapter dwells on some failures and abnormalities, not to criticize, but in an attempt to show court politics in action. By covering the period from 1700 (the accession of Sawai Jai Singh) to 1949 (the absorption of Jaipur state within the new Indian Union), the chapter also provides a chronology and a framework for the subsequent chapters.

Chapter Two, 'The Palace Buildings', describes how the various parts of the palace were built, added to and altered over the centuries, illustrating changes in the aesthetics and the developing needs of the occupants. Besides providing an architectural analysis of a historically important building complex, our intention here is to set the stage: to describe the spaces which provided the setting for the ritual and courtly activities described in later chapters. This chapter also includes our own plans of the Chandra Mahal (the oldest portion of the palace, never previously drawn up), together with some of the original architect's drawings, and discusses areas such as the women's quarters and the maharaja's private apartments that are not usually open to visitors.

The chapter on 'Festivals and Ceremonies' charts the annual calendar of religious festivals, paying special attention to how the role of the palace links it with the surrounding city. Drawing on two courtly texts from different periods – one composed in the 18th century, the other in the 20th century – it also describes royal birthdays and marriages, indicating how the form of these ceremonies developed or sustained traditions over time.

Woman playing a *vina*; Jaipur School, 18th century

The emphasis of Chapter Four, 'Artistic Identity,' lies on the production and consumption especially of the applied arts, such as metalwork, jewellery and textiles, and the promotion of Jaipur as a centre of trade in such items. We show how Jaipur's identity was forged quite deliberately on the back of its industrial arts and how its reputation as a good place to shop is neither recent nor arbitrary, but arose from aspects of court life and policy. The maharajas systematically encouraged the arts to give Jaipur a competitive edge amongst its neighbours. The chapter also discusses photography in Jaipur, which by the end of the 19th century was patronized and promoted in much the same ways as the city's longer established artistic media.

Chapter Five, 'Education and Sport,' covers both the role of these activities within the life of the palace and the part played by the court in promoting them in Jaipur state. It thus describes the evolving educational regime and curriculum of successive maharajas, from Mughal times to the modern era, and in turn their development of state education and sport.

The final chapter, on 'Governance', gives an account of the various departments of government that were housed within the palace and were responsible for the administration of everything from the maharaja's stables to agriculture and taxation in the Jaipur state. The chapter describes the evolution and periodic reform of these departments starting from the Mughal era up to the introduction of representative government.

One activity on which we have placed much less emphasis is warfare. Some readers might be surprised by this in view of the turbulent history of Rajasthan and the code of chivalry at the heart of the Rajput ethic. The proud and valorous Rajput warrior has long been a stock figure of Indian history. In a departure from this traditional emphasis we have chosen instead to focus on artistic and economic aspects, partly in order to show that there were other things going on in a Rajput court, and especially in the case of Jaipur where something out of the standard mould was contemplated by the rulers and their assistants from the outset.

There is another sense in which by implication we challenge standard historical accounts. The old adage about history being written by victors is true in many senses. The history of India in the late 19th and early 20th centuries is usually told as the story of the freedom movement, as a progress towards the undeniably crucial moment of Independence in 1947. In this narrative the former Indian or 'Princely' states are often depicted as having been obstacles: their people were seemingly apathetic, their rulers reluctant to surrender power and privilege for the greater good. Such an impression was reinforced by events in some states, such as Kashmir and Hyderabad, at the time of integration, and by the subsequent political opposition to the Congress posed by members of the former ruling families. The established caricature of the pampered, self-interested maharajas made it possible and even expedient for Indira Gandhi's administration to abolish their remaining vestiges of privilege in 1971.

Nationalist historians have tended to accept the Congress version of events, while foreign authors have mostly focussed on the big events and the successful political players,

such as Gandhi, Nehru and Patel. Only those with a special interest in the former Indian states have recognized that there is another story to tell. If there was less agitation in places like Jaipur this was because the chief aims of the freedom movement – self-government and statehood – were considered by its people to be already in place. Though formally under British suzerainty, Jaipur was a state governed by Indians, with its own legal system, penal code and armed forces. This book is in part a contribution to an attempt to understand the workings and the mind of one Indian administration before 1947.

Inside the Zanana Mahal

THE DYNASTIC SUCCESSION

The ten successive maharajas who ruled from the Jaipur City Palace were leaders of the Rajput clan known as the Kachchwahas. The members of this clan claimed descent from Kush, son of Rama, the hero of the *Ramayana*, and through him from the sun god Surya – hence their designation as *suryavanshi:* of the lineage of the Sun.

The distinguished 20th-century historian Sir Jadunath Sarkar wisely commented that it is best to leave the details of early genealogy to poets, bards and minstrels who specialized in such lore; we begin to reach what the historian would recognize as the solid ground of fact with the migration of this clan from their former territories around Gwalior towards Rajasthan in the 10th or 11th century. Their charismatic leader Dulha Rai, the 'bridegroom king', carved out a kingdom in the region known as Dhundhar by capturing the strongholds of the local tribes, the Minas and Bar-Gujars, who were subsequently co-opted as the watchmen and servants of the new state. At one point in his campaign, Dulha Rai very nearly suffered defeat at the hands of the Minas and was rescued only by the intervention of the goddess Jamwa Mata, to whom he therefore built a temple at the former Mina town of Manchi, renamed Ramgarh in honour of his divine ancestor. Dulha Rai's son and successor Kakil later succeeded in wresting Amber from the Minas and, as this position was more easily defensible, he made it the Kachchwaha capital in around 1070 A.D.

Already by this time northern India had begun to suffer a spate of invasions

An 18th-century representation of the temple of Jamwa-Mata at Ramgarh

Facing page:
An imaginary portrait of Kakilji, by the Indo-German artist A.H. Müller

The image of
Govind Dev,
originally enshrined
in a temple in
Vrindavan and now
in the temple in Jai
Niwas in Jaipur.
Here the *murti* is
dressed for the Teej
festival.

from across the Hindu Kush, and Kakil's descendants were to play prominent roles in the Rajput confederacies that attempted, unsuccessfully, to stem the tide. For example, Kakil's great-grandson, Pajvan, was related by marriage to Prithviraj Chauhan, traditionally regarded as the last Hindu king of Delhi, and fought alongside him at the battle of Tarain against the Afghan Muhammad of Ghor in 1192. Over three centuries later another Prithviraj – this one the leader of the Kachchwahas – similarly fought alongside Rana Sanga of Mewar against the Mughal conqueror Babur at the Battle of Khanua in 1527. But Prithviraj Kachchwaha's legacy to his clan was not only one of defeat, for his *rajguru* or spiritual preceptor had given him two sacred *murtis* that were to be cherished by his descendants. One was of Narasimha, which was housed in an ancient palace in the town of Amber. The other was of Sitaramji, later installed in a temple in Jaipur and traditionally carried ahead of the Jaipur army in battle.

Following the Mughal conquest and the death of Prithviraj, the Amber dynasty underwent a period of turbulence that was concluded only by the strategic alliance established with the new power by Bhar Mal (r. 1548-74). By securing the safe release of a besieged Mughal governor of Narnaul, Bhar Mal attracted the sympathetic attention of the young Emperor Akbar and was invited to court in December 1556. Later Bhar Mal played host in turn to Akbar, receiving him at Sanganer in January 1562, and offering the emperor his daughter in marriage. The solemnization of this wedding, which took place at Sambhar the following month, was the first of a series of marital alliances with the Mughal imperial family. For Akbar, it was vital either to win over or to subdue the Rajput clans, both to lessen the chances of revolt within his rapidly expanding empire and to secure control of the trade routes to the western seaports of Gujarat. For the Rajputs, the switch in policy from resistance to support offered a more stable future and opportunities for distinguished service.

No one took greater advantage of this change than the Kachchwaha leader Man Singh. Even as a young prince he was entrusted with commanding the imperial armies against the celebrated Rana Pratap of Mewar, who had chosen the path of continued resistance. Their encounter at the famous (if inconclusive) Battle of Haldighat in June 1576 marked merely the beginning of Man Singh's long career in imperial service, a career that stretched over nearly 40 years and saw him acting either as campaign manager or as governor in the Punjab, Afghanistan, Bihar, Orissa, Bengal and the Deccan. Apart from the acknowledgement of Mughal sovereignty, the price paid by Man Singh for this service was his almost continuous absence from his home state, but the prize won was the raising of the profile of that state within Indian polity.

Man Singh's legacy, like that of Prithviraj, also included the provision of two more cult images that were to be central to the religious practice of his descendants and their subjects. He brought from Bengal an image of Shila Devi and installed it in a temple within the new palace that he had begun to build in Amber. And at Vrindavan, the

heartland of the Braj country, he commissioned the building of the Govind Dev temple to enshrine the murti of Krishna that had been discovered by Roop Goswami, a disciple of the great sage Chaitanya.

Three generations later, Man Singh's career was played out again, this time for the benefit of Shah Jahan and Aurangzeb, by Jai Singh I (r. 1621-67). The so-called 'Mirza Raja' spent almost every year of his long reign on campaign, fighting for the Mughal cause everywhere from Central Asia in the north-west to the Deccan in the south and Monghyr in the east. In the last years of his life this veteran commander was responsible for the defeat and arrest of the Maratha leader Shivaji.

These, then, were the forebears of the maharajas of Jaipur. The men who founded the state and who forged the diplomatic alliance with the Mughals represented an inspiring example and a formidable inheritance to the rulers who followed.

The Dynastic Process

In theory, strict rules of inheritance governed the process of dynastic succession but, in practice, the transition from one reign to another was not always as orderly and uncontested as the rules were designed to make it. For example, Jagat Singh, the elder son of the great Man Singh, predeceased his father, leaving behind a son of his own, Maha Singh, who was – according to Rajput convention – the legitimate heir on the death of his grandfather in 1614. However the claims of this youth were passed over on the orders of the Mughal Emperor Jahangir in favour of his uncle – Man Singh's younger son, Bhau Singh – whom

The town of Sanganer is famous for its textile industry and its Jain temples.

Jahangir knew personally and trusted. Bhau Singh was therefore the officially recognized ruler from 1614 until his death in 1621. When he died without issue, the legitimate line – the progeny of Jagat – was reinstated but, as Maha Singh himself had died in 1617, it was his son, Jai Singh, who became the next raja. Many years later, in the genealogical section of a court poem entitled *Pratap Prakash*, the poet includes in the list of rulers both Jagat Singh and Maha Singh (who were born in the legitimate line but did not in fact rule) and omits any reference to Bhau Singh, the raja appointed by the diktat of the emperor. So the succession could be altered even retrospectively to legitimize or strengthen particular interested parties. Bhau Singh was reinstated in the record in the late 19th century.

The following account of the Jaipur dynasty focusses on the moments of transition from one ruler to another and on the efforts of successive maharajas to secure their hold on power. The main events and achievements of their reigns are described at greater length in later chapters; the emphasis here is on the process of succession. It is not our intention to revive long-abandoned claims, nor to question the legitimacy of any ruler, but to show that the process of succession was a complex and controversial one, and that a simple list or genealogical table would obscure more than it would reveal. For good or ill the disputes were settled and no useful purpose could be served by attempting to reopen them. Besides, Jaipur was far from unique in suffering them: legal challenges and even fratricide pepper the annals of every ruling dynasty. But exploring the nature of such events, in the case of Jaipur, helps to explain why certain reigns took the course they did.

Sawai Jai Singh II (r. 1699-1743)

Between Jai Singh I and his illustrious descendant and namesake, Sawai Jai Singh II, the succession proceeded by primogeniture and according to protocol, without intervention from uncles, though again with the omission of one generation (as Ram Singh – son of Jai Singh I – was succeeded by his grandson Vishnu Singh). Even so, Sawai Jai Singh II's grip on power was far from secure in the early years of his reign. His first problem was his youth: having been born in 1688, he was only eleven years old when his father Vishnu Singh died at the end of 1699. Later he had to marshal the support of all of his *thakurs* (nobles) to dismiss a challenge from a younger half-brother who had gained Mughal backing in his efforts to unseat him.

But by far his greatest setback was his disastrous entanglement in the Mughal war of succession that followed on the death of Aurangzeb in 1707. In accordance with the long-established practice of his ancestors, the young Sawai Jai Singh had taken employment in the empire and was serving under the command of the Mughal prince Azam Shah. He therefore felt bound to support Azam Shah's bid for the imperial throne against his brothers. But the bid was unsuccessful and the victor in the dispute – Prince Muazzam, who took the throne as Emperor Bahadur Shah – punished the allies of his rivals, including Sawai Jai Singh, by dispossessing them of their kingdoms. So the young raja had at last come of age only to find that he had no state to rule. With the help of the

Maharana of Udaipur he was able to recover control of Amber by the autumn of 1708, but he was not able to normalize his relations with the Mughal authorities until after the death of Bahadur Shah in 1712. Moreover, the terms of the treaty that he had made with Udaipur stored up problems regarding his own succession for the future.

On the surface, Sawai Jai Singh's appointment as *subahdar* (governor) of the Mughal province of Malwa from 1712-16 looked like business as usual and he enjoyed a position of trust at the court of the Mughal Emperor Muhammad Shah (r. 1719-48). But beneath the semblance of normality Mughal power was waning and the authority of the emperor in particular was greatly diminished. In this changed environment Sawai Jai Singh ambitiously asserted his own claims on regional authority and refashioned his state as an alternative power base. Moving his capital from the old fortified retreat at Amber to the newly constructed commercial city of Jaipur in 1727-34 was a part of this process. If his forebears Man Singh and Jai Singh I had raised the status of their kingdom during the heyday of Mughal power, Sawai Jai Singh II re-invented it for a period of Mughal decline and sought to give it a leading role in the emerging new order.

Sawai Jai Singh is remembered in history chiefly as the founder of Jaipur – a city that is renowned both for its architectural beauty and for its commercial success – and as an astronomer who built five observatories and reformed the Hindu calendar. It might in fairness be said that he cannot take sole credit for either achievement as he was ably assisted in the first by his prime minister, Vidyadhar, and in the second by a south Indian pandit named Jagannath. But his vision in promoting these projects is beyond dispute. That vision is reflected in his religious practice as well. He sponsored the performance of a number of ancient Vedic rituals, including the Vajpey Yajna (a rite which entails offering *soma*, made from the juice of a creeper, to the gods) and the Ashvamedh (or horse sacrifice); and by these means he reinforced his claims to be regarded as *samrat*, paramount amongst Hindu kings of his era. On a less arcane and more popular level, he brought into the state the murti of Govind Devji (displaced when its temple in Vrindavan was partially destroyed) and established it in a new temple in Jaipur as a major cult image in the devotions of his subjects.

During his lifetime he enjoyed a reputation as one of the most powerful and influential men in India. On his death in 1743 at the age of fifty-four, he bequeathed to his successors a state which was amongst the most dynamic in all matters of religion, learning and trade.

Ishvari Singh (r. 1743-50) and Madho Singh I (r. 1750-68)

In view of the strength of this legacy, it is scarcely surprising that there should have been competition for the control of it, and unfortunately Sawai Jai Singh also left behind the seeds of a legal dispute. His first born son, Shiv Singh, had died young and so he was succeeded by his eldest surviving son, Ishvari Singh, then aged twenty-two. This unfortunate prince was immediately challenged by his younger half-brother Madho Singh

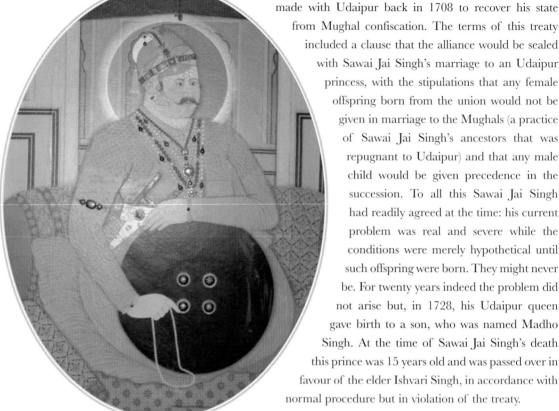

Maharaja Madho
Singh I; portrait by
Sahib Ram

whose legal ground was the treaty that Sawai Jai Singh had made with Udaipur back in 1708 to recover his state from Mughal confiscation. The terms of this treaty included a clause that the alliance would be sealed with Sawai Jai Singh's marriage to an Udaipur princess, with the stipulations that any female offspring born from the union would not be given in marriage to the Mughals (a practice of Sawai Jai Singh's ancestors that was repugnant to Udaipur) and that any male child would be given precedence in the succession. To all this Sawai Jai Singh had readily agreed at the time: his current problem was real and severe while the conditions were merely hypothetical until such offspring were born. They might never be. For twenty years indeed the problem did not arise but, in 1728, his Udaipur queen gave birth to a son, who was named Madho Singh. At the time of Sawai Jai Singh's death this prince was 15 years old and was passed over in favour of the elder Ishvari Singh, in accordance with normal procedure but in violation of the treaty.

The decision of the Maharana of Udaipur to support Madho Singh's claim with force of arms was prompted by more than loyalty to a young relative and dogged adherence to the treaty: he was no doubt motivated in part by a desire to undermine the power and authority of the Jaipur state which, by having pursued strategic alliances with the Mughals rather than a policy of isolationism, had surpassed the traditionally pre-eminent state of Udaipur in both wealth and influence.

Though Ishvari Singh enjoyed the support of his *thakurs* he was vulnerable. It was not enough for him to sit tight and defend his position. To make his accession fully secure he was bound to pay a duty call on the Mughal emperor. A legal complication that always beset Rajput-Mughal relations was that while the Hindu rajas, such as the rulers of Amber-Jaipur, regarded the land that they controlled as a birthright (*watan*), the Mughals considered it as belonging ultimately to their crown (*khalsa*), to which it automatically reverted on a raja's death, to be given back to the raja's heir at the emperor's discretion, as a leasehold (*jagir*). So it was not sufficient for a raja to be accepted as the legal heir by his *thakurs*; if he wished to be regarded as such by the world outside his borders he had to be appointed or confirmed as the ruler by the emperor. And for this, he had to go to court and ask.

Ishvari Singh deferred this necessary visit for a year, apprehensive about what might occur in his absence from Jaipur. His fears proved justified: as soon as his back was turned, Madho Singh and his allies made their move. On this occasion they failed to unseat him because of some skilful handling by the commander-in-chief of Ishvari Singh's forces; and they failed when they tried again in 1747, despite the additional support of Maratha forces which had been drawn into the alliance. But their persistent efforts were eventually successful: repeated attacks or threats of attack finally demoralized Ishvari Singh and when they approached the city in 1750, he made no attempt to defend it and retreated to his private apartments where he took his own life.

The cremation sites of Rajput rulers and heroes are customarily marked by *chhatris* or pavilions. Those commemorating the former rulers of Amber are clustered on a royal cremation ground at the edge of that city, but following the transfer of the capital this place was no longer used, and on the death of Sawai Jai Singh a new cremation ground was established just to the north of Jaipur, at Gaitor. However, uniquely among the rulers of Jaipur, Ishvari Singh was not cremated here but at a spot within the boundary wall of the palace grounds, at the south-west corner of the Tal Katora. His forced suicide gave Ishvari Singh a special status among his later successors and his *chhatri* became, along with certain temples near the palace, one of a number of sites of obligatory *puja* by the ruling maharaja on certain specified occasions.

The court poet who passed in silence over the reign of Bhau Singh ignored Ishvari Singh likewise, while a French commentator in the 1790s, who did not witness these events but reported them from hearsay, denounced him as 'indolent,' and some historians have judged him 'deficient'. But, in fairness, he was merely the victim of those who were jealous of his inheritance, and the regular ritual visits to his *chhatri* by later rulers have elevated his action from a disgrace to something that demands reverence.

His half-brother Madho Singh was literally led to the *gaddi* by the Maratha chief Malhar Rao Holkar, who did not long remain an ally. The Marathas had supported his cause not out of generosity or respect for treaties but with the hope of financial gain, and their haggling over how much they believed they were now owed quickly soured their relations with the newly installed ruler. When Madho Singh in his turn came

Maharaja Ishvari Singh; portrait by Sahib Ram

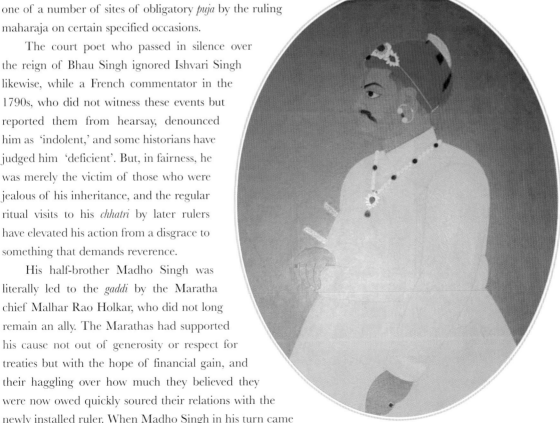

to make his courtesy call on the emperor he too had to watch his back, but the threat he feared came from his former allies. The populace of Jaipur shared his disgust and, in January 1751, they rose in a body and massacred several hundred Maratha soldiers who were swaggering about the city and behaving – so it was thought – rather too much like an army of occupation, too little like privileged visitors.

From this moment onwards, throughout the 18 years of his reign, Madho Singh had to defend his state repeatedly against Maratha incursions. That he succeeded in repelling them more often with bribes than with arms is a measure not only of the Marathas' greater military strength but also of their greater interest in cash than in conquest. Throughout the second half of the 18th century, Maratha depredations posed a constant threat to the older Rajput states, disrupting their politics and threatening ruin to their economies. But the Marathas never acted concertedly, as they might have done, to replace the Rajput states with an empire of their own, preferring to plunder and abandon rather than to settle and tax whatever land they overran.

Prithvi Singh (r. 1768-78) and Pratap Singh (r. 1778-1803)

Even by the standards of the 18th century – a time that was fraught with political dangers and the risk of disease – the Jaipur maharajas did not live long. Madho Singh I died at the age of just forty, making him, apart from Sawai Jai Singh, the most long-lived in the period before the political settlements and the medical advances of the late 19th century.

He was succeeded by his son Prithvi Singh, then aged five. This succession was normal and according to custom. What was remarkable was that the person appointed as regent to rule on behalf of this minor was not the boy's own mother but another of the late Madho Singh's queens, who was a member of the Chundawat clan from Deogarh in Mewar, and who had a son of her own, Prithvi's younger half-brother Pratap. She took as her principal advisers a man named Firuz, who had formerly been an elephant driver and was widely believed to be her illicit lover, and her own father, who came over from Deogarh for the purpose.

The *thakurs* of the Jaipur court were appalled by

this outside interference, by female rule and by their own loss of influence. So they attempted – as was their right and indeed their duty according to Rajput custom – to overthrow this unconventional regency; but being divided into two squabbling factions with differing ideas about what should take its place, they failed, and soon began to focus their energies instead on consolidating their personal authority in their individual *thikanas* or estates. Notably ambitious in this regard was the Rao of Macheri, who managed to enlarge his *thikana* on the eastern edge of the state and even gained recognition for himself from Delhi as an independent raja, thus sowing the seed of what was to become the state of Alwar. The legacy of Sawai Jai Singh was beginning to fragment.

After 10 years, Prithvi Singh suddenly died as a result of a fall from his horse. He was then 15 and not far short of an age when he might have dispensed with the regent and her advisers and assumed control himself. He was already married and the father of an infant prince named Man Singh. But when he fell to his death the queen regent managed to install on the *gaddi* her own son, Prithvi's younger half-brother Pratap Singh. This manoeuvre must arouse the suspicion that Prithvi Singh's fall was engineered to secure the continuation of the power of the regency faction. For the second time in as many generations, a younger brother had wrested control (or had it wrested on his behalf) through foul play. But again there was a general acquiescence, especially after Pratap Singh was officially recognized as maharaja by the Mughal emperor in February 1779.

The unscrupulous mahout Firuz did not long survive the change of puppet: he was murdered when he unwisely became entangled in affairs between the assertive Rao of Macheri and the Mughal commander-in-chief. The scheming queen mother died soon after, clearing the way for Pratap to emerge from his minority and claim full powers. His reign of 25 years was the longest that Jaipur had seen since the days of Sawai Jai Singh. It was a period plagued as usual by conflict with the Marathas, but one that was characterized too by the further development of Jaipur's arts and industries, ensuring that some aspects of the founder's legacy were remembered and revived.

One event that blemished the latter years of Pratap Singh's reign – and which, according to a local superstition, influenced the dynastic succession – concerned Jaipur's

Maharaja Pratap Singh; portrait by Sahib Ram

Facing page: Maharaja Prithvi Singh; detail from a contemporary Mughal-style portrait

first diplomatic contact with the British in 1799. By this time the British were well established in eastern and southern India, but they had as yet little influence in the central and western parts of upper India (before their capture of Delhi and Agra in 1803). Wazir Ali, whom they had deposed as Nawab of Avadh, took his revenge by murdering the Resident and other British officials in Banaras; and when he was pursued, sought sanctuary in Jaipur. The British demand that he be surrendered to them violated Rajput customs of hospitality and at first the Jaipur court stoutly refused. But cautiously regarding the British strength of arms, Pratap Singh eventually relented and handed over custody of his embarrassing guest. Though politically prudent, this departure from custom cost Jaipur much loss of prestige. According to legend, the fugitive Wazir Ali's mother cursed the dynastic line by expressing the fervent hope that henceforth all successive maharajas of Jaipur would die as soon as a son and heir was born to them.

Jagat Singh (r.1803-18) and Jai Singh III (r. 1819-35)

The curse did not affect Pratap Singh as he already had a teenage son who came to the *gaddi* as Maharaja Jagat Singh on his father's death in 1803. But the curse may have been remembered by Jagat: certainly later generations attributed his failure to produce a legitimate heir during the sixteen years of his reign to his supposed unwillingness to put it to the test.

The more obvious fallout from the Wazir Ali affair was the bad start to relations with the British and, in this regard, things did not soon improve. In the first year of his reign Jagat Singh was offered, and accepted, a 'subsidiary alliance', which afforded Jaipur some protection from its traditional enemies at the cost of recognizing the authority of the British as a new regional power. Because of changes in policy in Calcutta, however, the British themselves quickly repudiated this agreement, though it was unequally weighted in their own favour, thus deepening the distrust on the Jaipur side. British policy changed again, with fresh instructions from London to renew the link, but it was not until 1818 that Jaipur overcame its suspicions and followed the example of neighbouring Rajput states by entering into a new and permanent treaty.

Whether it was the result of his superstition or of some other cause, Jagat Singh's death without issue at the end of 1818 precipitated the most serious constitutional crisis to date. On previous occasions there had been one too many claimants for the throne; this time it seemed there was one too few. Rajput convention provided for such eventualities through the mechanism of adoption. In Jaipur, as in other Rajput states, certain families closely related to the ruling line were identified as the preferred source of adopted heirs. On this occasion, as the adoption had not been made by the maharaja himself before his death, it was the duty of the *thakurs* to oversee the operation according to the prescribed rules. But it seems that procedure in Jagat Singh's court was not as well regulated as it might have been, the most influential figure there being the chief eunuch, Mohan Nazir, who took it upon himself to select a candidate of his own liking. Though a Rajput and of noble birth, the nine-year-old boy he chose was not a member of any of the specified families and had no conceivable claim; nor did Mohan Nazir have any right to make the decision. But the eunuch persuaded the British authorities to support his action and to issue a letter recognizing the boy as the legitimate ruler – an intervention by the paramount power that was not only ill-informed on matters of Rajput law but which contravened one of the clauses of their own treaty, which specified that they would not interfere in the dynastic succession.

This situation was intolerable alike to the *thakurs*, whose function had been by-passed, and to the ladies of the *zanana*, languishing under the tyrannous regime of Mohan Nazir and his young puppet. One of the ladies, a queen of the late maharaja, offered a solution to the problem by declaring that she was pregnant: that Jagat Singh was going to have an heir after all. The events that followed her implausible declaration reveal the power of two conventions on which she was relying. First, in spite of the importance of the matter, the rules of *parda* could not be suspended, and the *thakurs* had to leave it to the other women of the *zanana* to verify her claim to be pregnant and in due course to witness the birth of a posthumous son. Secondly, when in April 1819 the women announced that all was as it should be, the *thakurs* gave their consent. Any doubt that might have been entertained in suspicious minds about whether the infant they were presented with was really the legitimate child of Jagat Singh became irrelevant, because the *thakurs'* acceptance of him was alone sufficient to make him the legal heir. He was given the name Jai Singh III and recognized as their ruler. Mohan Nazir and his young pretender were quietly removed and the British authorities were obliged to revoke their earlier stance and acquiesce in the fait accompli.

The solution to the crisis was no doubt welcome, but at the time it must have struck many as more satisfactory for the medium than for the short term, since in the immediate future the enthronement of an infant entailed another period of minority rule, with a queen mother acting as regent and pulling strings from behind the *parda*. As in the days of Prithvi Singh, the *thakurs* often found themselves outmanoeuvred by the dubious individuals whom the queen mother appointed as her ministers, unable even to gain access to their clansman and lord, much less to offer him counsel according to their historic function. So

Maharaja Jagat Singh; portrait by Sahib Ram

25

they tended to retreat to their thikanas to bide their time, waiting for their young maharaja to come of age.

He never did. Jai Singh III never had a chance to live up to the proud name he had inherited. He died in 1835 at the age of 16, without having emerged from the close confinement in which his mother's chief minister had kept him all his life. But he did at least leave behind an incontestably legitimate son and heir: the two-year-old Ram Singh II. And this child was to turn out to be a greater legacy than anyone could then have even hoped for.

Ram Singh II (r. 1835-1880) and Madho Singh II (r. 1880-1922)

The death of Jai Singh III at an age when he might have been ready to break free from his guardians looked to some suspiciously like a repetition of the events of the earlier period of regency rule, when Prithvi Singh had mysteriously fallen off his horse at the age of 15. The *thakurs* openly accused the queen's minister Jhuta Ram of having poisoned the young maharaja and, backed by popular resentment, they succeeded in ousting him. Of course they had to reconcile themselves to plunging without break into yet another period of minority rule, with its inevitable machinery of a regency council and an overbearing mother. They would have to wait for a further period of 16 years before they could expect to sit in *darbar* with their ruler and help him to guide the fortunes of their state, though it had already suffered neglect and misrule for long enough.

But things did not turn out as badly as they might have feared, with help coming from a surprising quarter. The British were taking an increasing interest in the affairs of the Rajput states, and in 1839 they assumed control of the regency council in Jaipur by appointing their own political agent or Resident as its chairman. Far from marginalizing the *thakurs* this move brought them closer to power. The British understanding of the constitution of the Rajput states, although it was perhaps influenced as much by English medieval history as by Rajput realities, placed great importance on feudal hierarchies and ancestral rights and thus tended to include the *thakurs*, who were seen as 'barons', amongst those who should properly exercise authority. The British also shared the *thakurs*' view of the desirability of excluding so far as possible the influence of the *zanana*, to the chagrin of the queen mother or Maji, who was keen to fulfil her traditional role as an irresponsible *eminence grise*.

John Ludlow, who served as British Resident in Jaipur in the mid-1840s, went further and assumed responsibility for the education of the young maharaja, equipping him for government by ensuring he had a firm grounding in politics and natural sciences as well as the traditional religious and language studies. When he came of age, in 1851, Maharaja Ram Singh II was given full ruling powers and the regency council was disbanded but the habit persisted of depending on the wise counsel of his more astute *thakurs* and on British allegiance. His response to the first major crisis showed that his education had 'taken': he supported the British during the Rebellion of 1857, in so far as the events of that trauma

Facing page: Maharaja Ram Singh II; hand-coloured photograph by T. Murray

27

touched his borders, by giving sanctuary and safe escort to Europeans fleeing from Delhi and by denying passage across his lands to mutinous sepoys.

The last two decades of Ram Singh's reign were devoted to the modernization of Jaipur. The state that his ancestor, Sawai Jai Singh II, had previously refashioned at the end of the Mughal era was now reformed again at the beginning of the Victorian British Empire. The most conspicuous of a broad range of advances were made in the fields of state education, health and communications, and in the further development of Jaipur's traditional arts and industries. The city spilled out beyond its old fortified walls, with the rapid proliferation of public buildings, parks and new institutions of work and leisure. Every new civic amenity that the 19th century had invented was duly provided by an enlightened and industrious maharaja.

The only thing that Ram Singh did not supply was a son and heir. The reason for this omission is not clear, as commentators at the time tended to focus instead on the process by which Ram Singh selected a candidate for adoption. It was only when he was dying at the age of 47, that Ram Singh named his successor. He was bound by convention to choose someone from within the Rajawat branch of the Kachchwaha clan, but there were so many subdivisions of this clan that any choice was bound to arouse some envy and resentment, if not open challenge, and Ram Singh perhaps delayed his announcement until the imminence of his own death made it essential, to minimize the period of fuss.

One account of how he came to make his choice begins by recalling how some years earlier Ram Singh had been required to settle a succession dispute in one of the state's *thikanas*. When Raghunath Singh, the Thakur of Isarda, died, he left two sons whose mothers quarrelled over which of them was the rightful heir to the father's title. Ram Singh canvassed the views of the other *thakurs* and agreed with the majority view amongst them; but when he announced this decision he offered some words of consolation to the disappointed younger brother, Kayam Singh, by suggesting that one day he might after all have a *gaddi* of his own, a more significant one than Isarda's. This enigmatic remark now became clear (or his prophecy was fulfilled) as Ram Singh named this same Kayam Singh as heir to the *gaddi* of Jaipur itself.

A slightly different version of events was later recorded by Thakur Amar Singh of Kanota, a descendant of Ram Singh's last chief minister. 'Ram Singhji had not adopted anyone until he was on his deathbed,' Amar Singh recalled, and 'when there was no hope of his life, my grand uncle, Thakur Fateh Singhji, the then minister, asked the Maharaja as to whom he intended to adopt. The Maharaja said, "Whomever you choose and the government approves of." Hearing this, my grandfather and his two brothers chose the present Maharaja who was the younger brother of the Thakur of Isarda'. Asked why this young man was considered a suitable candidate, Amar Singh said 'because he was of a major age which would mean there would not be a regency for long. Then having seen a lot of adversity he knew something of the world and also had a little education'.

Whichever version is closer to the truth it is clear that Ram Singh had met the young Kayam Singh at the time of the death of the boy's father and he had taken some

notice of his subsequent career – which had indeed been less than pampered since his disappointment in Isarda. Avoiding a regency was no longer so obviously a virtue: after all, Ram Singh's long schooling had prepared him well for kingship, while Amar Singh was quite right to describe Kayam Singh's early education as 'little,' for it had been decidedly intermittent. The most prominent activity on his curriculum had been wrestling. But he was a young man of courage and experience. He was 19 years old when adopted and on attaining the *gaddi* he took the name and title Maharaja Madho Singh II.

His reign of four decades carried Jaipur into the 20th century as he and his ministers (especially Babu Kanti Chander Mukerjee) continued and expanded the progressive policies of Ram Singh. Madho Singh II was a more controversial figure than his predecessor and was not universally praised. Some of the *thakurs* found him temperamental, while some among the city's intellectual classes considered him ill-educated. The British respected and

Maharaja Madho Singh II, towards the end of his life, with an entourage including (at the front on the right) the newly adopted Mormukut Singh

appreciated him for his loyalty and generosity – especially for his contributions towards the war effort during the First World War (1914-18) – but were put off by his religious orthodoxy: he refused, for example, to eat in company with foreigners. He remains an under-appreciated ruler, but one who walked the tightrope between tradition and modernity, and who negotiated his path through the hopes of competing factions with tact and innate sound judgment.

Man Singh II (r. 1922-49)

One respect in which Madho Singh II resembled his predecessor was in his failure to produce a legitimate son and heir. He fathered numerous sons by concubines but none by his legally married queens. This was a matter of public comment and some criticism: it was said that he neglected his queens and was noted that he built an extensive new suite of *zanana* apartments within the seclusion of Nahargarh, the fortress overlooking the city, to accommodate his favourite concubines away from palace scrutiny. Many believed that he purposefully avoided begetting an heir because he was fearful of the old curse put on the dynasty by Wazir Ali's mother.

Whatever the reason, he too was going to have to adopt. In an effort to avert controversy and squabbling, his first plan was to make his selection in secret and to send his candidate's name in a sealed envelope to the Viceroy with the request that it be made public only on his own death. But this strategy did not work. The Thakur of Jhalai believed that his own family stood first among the proper sources of adoption and, as he had not been consulted, he guessed that he had not been favoured and made known his discontent. The Maharaja was therefore urged by his advisers to hold a special *darbar* to announce his chosen successor publicly and officially install him as Maharaj Kumar, or heir apparent. This event duly took place on 24 March, 1921, and the heir was revealed to be again from Isarda: he was the Thakur of Isarda's second son, Mormukut Singh, who had been born in August 1911 and so was now nine years old.

Although the majority in Jaipur gave this information a dutiful welcome, the adoption could not immediately receive official sanction from the Viceroy because the Thakur of Jhalai, far from being silenced, declared his intention to mount a legal challenge. He gained the support of the influential Maharaja of Bikaner (a kinsman of his) and he engaged the support of the distinguished lawyer Tej Bahadur Sapru. The case would have to be settled.

Jaipur's treaty with the British Crown acknowledged the maharaja's right to adopt an heir 'according to Hindu law and to the customs of your race'. The point at issue was the precise nature of those 'customs'. Sapru's argument hinged on a passage in the work of the great historian of the Rajputs, James Tod, who in 1832 had recorded that in such matters the relevant branches of the Kachchwaha clan were the Rajawats. 'The Rajawats,' he explained, 'constitute a numerous frèrage [brotherhood], of which the Jhalai house takes the lead; and in which, provided there are no mental or physical disabilities, the right of

Facing page:
Maharaja Man Singh II with advisers, at the time of his first marriage, in 1924; hand-coloured photograph

furnishing heirs to the *gaddi* of Jaipur is a long-established, incontrovertible and inalienable privilege.' Sapru seized on this sentence as showing that the Jhalai family should be the first choice. Not so, responded the officials of the Mahakma Khas (the maharaja's private office), because the words 'in which' in the sentence quoted must refer to its main subject (that is to the 'frèrage' of Rajawats) and not to the Jhalai house, the subject of a sub-clause. Isarda is one of the Rajawat branches and is thus a legitimate source.

Plainly the Mahakma Khas were the better grammarians; but rather than depend on pedantry alone they went further and questioned whether Tod could be regarded as an authoritative source on matters relating to Jaipur. And they advanced another argument which was designed to fix the Thakur of Jhalai in a double bind. Any candidate for adoption, they insisted, had to be demonstrably of 'suitable demeanour and attitude'; and the Maharaja regarded Jhalai's challenge as a gesture of disloyalty to the state, thus showing his unfitness to rule it. In short, Jhalai's claim was in itself a disqualification.

With all of these arguments the Maharaja's officials won the day and the adoption of Mormukut Singh was confirmed by the Viceroy. With the death of his adoptive father 18 months later he ascended the *gaddi* as Maharaja Man Singh II, at the age of 11.

The prospect of yet another period of minority rule, which would last for the best part of a decade, was dismaying to some Jaipur citizens. A professor of history at the Maharaja's College, for example, grumbled in a newspaper article that 'the uncertainty about the future has spread gloom over the city'. But such fears were exaggerated: as the professor himself admitted, the state by now employed many capable people well suited

Maharaja Man Singh II with *pujaris*, preparing to celebrate his Silver Jubilee in 1947

to guide its fortunes in the interval, while the young Maharaja was educated, first at Mayo College and then at the military academy in Woolwich, in England.

From the moment of his investiture with full ruling powers in 1931, Man Singh II was an immensely popular ruler. His predecessors had commanded loyalty, but of a sort that was due as much to the office as to the man; while in the case of Man Singh it was a response to his personal energy and charisma, which inspired devotion among his subjects and won him admirers abroad. And yet events elsewhere in India were to ensure that he was to be Jaipur's last independent ruling maharaja.

Within British India proper – the regions that Britain ruled directly – agitation for independence steadily gained momentum in the years after the First World War; but initially this had comparatively little impact on the Indian (or 'Princely') States such as Jaipur. There, the political aspirations of the people, in so far as they existed, were addressed to the maharaja and his ministers. Why agitate for Indian rule and for statehood when both were already firmly in place? The Congress regarded the maharajas and their complacent citizens as obstacles and distractions, and nationalist historians have tended to follow their cue in depicting princely rule as reactionary – but these are views from the other side of an important political divide.

More recent and sympathetic observers have been more mindful of the once autonomous agency of the Indian states. Individual maharajas might either welcome or deplore the efforts of the Congress within British India (most of them, it is true, were mistrustful); but until the very last moments of British rule they continued to assume – and to be assured – that any

Maharaja Man Singh II in army uniform with Maharani Gayatri Devi

change would not fundamentally alter the integrity of their own states. The question before them was what new relationship would subsist between their states and a Congress-ruled former British India? They expected to become parts of some new confederation, with continuing links to the British Crown as enshrined in their treaties. In any such confederation, they supposed, their borders and dynastic succession would remain intact. This was no anachronistic delusion on their part: the Government of India Act of 1935 invited their responses to a draft 'Instrument of Accession' which defined the continuing powers of their states' governments, in relation to those of the projected federal government.

The idea of a confederation that would include the states as autonomous units was scuppered by the maharajas' collective failure to agree on the terms of the relationship and by the realization that the treaties with the Crown would be unsustainable following the British departure. This left the states with no option but to dissolve themselves and become integrated into the new Indian Union. Even this process required negotiation and was not completed in the case of Jaipur until 1949, two years after Independence. But with integration accomplished, the rule of the maharajas ended.

Jaipur was amalgamated with the neighbouring Rajput kingdoms to create the new state officially called Rajasthan (a name that had previously been used, as an alternative to 'Rajputana', as an informal description of the region). That Jaipur city was selected as the capital of this enlarged state is a measure of its standing and prestige as much as a function of geography. Likewise, Man Singh II was granted the new title 'Rajpramukh', making him the titular head of Rajasthan, with the idea that its new political leaders – the democratically elected ministers and their officials – would work closely with him, as they built new institutions. The title soon turned out to be a hollow crown: a gesture of appeasement rather than the symbol of a sincere aspiration. Like other former maharajas, Man Singh retained a strong hold over the affections of his former subjects but he quickly learnt that if he wished to exert any influence it could only be by holding office.

In fact it was his youngest wife, Maharani Gayatri Devi, who stood for election, becoming an MP for the opposition Swatantra Party in 1962. Man Singh himself was nominated to the Rajya Sabha, the upper house of the national parliament, and was appointed as India's Ambassador to Spain in 1965, but he was increasingly excluded from any political role in his own former state. He died from a heart attack in June 1970, whilst playing polo in England. As he was still fit and active, his death seemed tragically early, but at fifty-eight he had in fact lived longer than any of the preceding maharajas of Jaipur.

Brigadier Bhawani Singh

Ironically, given that both he and his predecessor were adopted, Man Singh II, who had no state to bequeath, had four legitimate sons. The title passed to the eldest of them, Bhawani Singh (born in 1931), and with it control of the 'privy purse', the financial compensation that had been awarded to the maharajas when they surrendered their powers and the states' incomes. Even these residual tokens were not to last much longer. In a populist move devised

to raise her electoral appeal, the Prime Minister Indira Gandhi abolished royal titles and privy purses in 1971. Apart from being a breach of faith, this action failed as the socialist measure it was canvassed as, because – as many at the time pointed out – by this date the steadily diminishing privy purses were mostly consumed in paying the pensions of former palace employees. Bhawani Singh was in any event scarcely living the life of a maharaja: he had opted instead for a career in the Indian army, where he rose to the rank of Brigadier and was awarded the MVC for distinguished service during the Bangladesh war of 1971. While a few ex-maharajas in this period sat in crumbling palaces bemoaning change, the more enterprising, like Bhawani Singh, sought alternative occupation and service, which often took them (like their ancestors in Mughal times) far away from their ancestral homelands. Their understandable distrust of some sectors of the government was not soothed by the further humiliations meted out to them during the Emergency declared by Indira Gandhi in 1975. Both Bhawani Singh and Gayatri Devi were briefly incarcerated in Tihar Jail on charges that might fairly be called trumped up, while their properties were raided by income tax officials.

Since his retirement from the army, Bhawani Singh has devoted his energies to the charitable trust that owns and manages the museum and the City Palace (part of which is his home). The work of that trust makes the matter of succession and inheritance a continuing one, even if the dynastic element is absent. This explains why in 2002 Bhawani Singh and his wife, Maharani Padmini Devi, being without a son, formally adopted as heir their grandson Padmanabh, elder son of their only daughter. So far as can be assured, for the foreseeable future, the descendants of the last ruling maharaja will continue to hold in trust the legacy of Sawai Jai Singh.

Maharaja Bhawani Singh

THE PALACE BUILDINGS

When it was selected as the site for the new city of Jaipur in 1727, the open plain to the south of Amber already had a few pre-existing structures and features. Amongst these was a hunting lodge and formal garden known as Jai Niwas, which had been built for Sawai Jai Singh as early as 1713, according to a contemporary court text entitled *Sawai Jai Singh Charit*. When giving orders for the planning of the new capital, Sawai Jai Singh specified quite expressly that Jai Niwas was to be included within its walls. The importance of Jai Niwas by this date was no longer as a royal pleasure resort, for soon after its construction it had acquired a different function and significance, as the shrine of the *murti* of Govind Dev.

This important image, representing Krishna as the young cowherd, had been given to Sawai Jai Singh's ancestor, Raja Man Singh, by a disciple of the saint Chaitanya; and it was first installed in 1590 in a temple built by Man Singh for the purpose in Vrindavan, the town that had been identified by Chaitanya as the scene of Krishna's youth. Later, in 1669, anticipating an attack on the temple ordered by the Mughal emperor Aurangzeb, the *murti* was hastily removed and kept in hiding. For over 40 years it was transferred from one secret location to another, rarely emerging to public view for the benefit of its devotees. Its movements were kept so strictly confidential that it is impossible now to reconstruct them with certainty. But in 1713 Sawai Jai Singh had it brought to Amber and, throwing off the veil of concealment, installed it in a temple outside the city in a garden named Kanak Vrindavan, in honour of its starting point. Shortly thereafter, probably in 1715, it was moved again to its current resting place in Jai Niwas.

The reason for this final move is not entirely clear. A local legend states that the god appeared to Sawai Jai Singh in a dream, demanding residence in Jai Niwas. It is equally possible that it was a pre-emptive move, intended to prepare the ground for the later construction of the city around the site. The new capital, designed all at once and almost from scratch, was laid out according to traditional Indic principles of architecture (principles that are recorded in canonical treatises known as *vastu shastras*). One of these principles holds that a royal capital should have the palace at the centre, which should in turn contain a temple dedicated to Vishnu. Govind Dev is of course an *avatar* of Vishnu. So, whether it was by accident or by premeditated design, Jai Niwas – containing a suitable temple and surrounded by an otherwise undeveloped plain – presented itself as an ideal spot for the foundation of the city.

This explains Sawai Jai Singh's insistence that Jai Niwas should be included in the city. It also explains the subsequent development of the garden and its temple as the heart of the palace compound, and the dedication of the entire central plot of the city to these and other palace buildings. The palace as a whole occupies an area of approximately one square kilometre in the city centre and is contained within a boundary wall, or *sarahad*. The temple, located at its core, was (and remains) the one part of the compound that

Facing page:
One of the four painted gates in the Pritam Niwas Chowk

37

was readily accessible to all the citizens. God, king and people were thus brought together in a single ritual space. To be further sure that the association between himself and the popular cult image was evident to his subjects, Sawai Jai Singh declared that the god was the real ruler of the state (often therefore addressed simply as '*Thakurji*') while he himself was merely the *diwan* or minister.

This history makes it tempting to identify the Govind Dev temple not only with the site but with the very fabric of the original hunting lodge. It is clear however that the temple has been rebuilt (first in 1735) and subsequently added to, even in recent times, albeit in ways that maintain its unusual appearance, more reminiscent of a garden-palace than of temple architecture (comparisons might be made with the roughly contemporary pavilions of the Dilaram Bagh below the palace at Amber, and the palace of the Jat leader Suraj Mal at Dig).

The garden in which the temple stands was probably also redesigned when the area was developed as the palace compound. Its form is a double *char-bagh*. The temple occupies a terrace between two square gardens, each of which is subdivided into four by water channels that bisect it and meet at a fountain in the centre. This *char-bagh* pattern originated in Persia and was introduced into India by the early Mughals. There is ample literary evidence that traditional Indian palaces, including ancient ones that are now lost and beyond the reach even of archaeology, contained pleasure gardens; but obviously they did not follow this distinctively Persian-Mughal plan. In view of Sawai Jai Singh's efforts – through his religious practice and literary patronage – to assert his identity as a Hindu king, and his desire to present a resurgent Rajput state as a challenge to the waning

The Govind Dev temple in Jai Niwas, from the top of the Chandra Mahal; on the left of the picture is the roof of the banquet hall, and on the right is the Kamal Burj.

power of the Mughals, this note of Mughal influence that is struck by the garden might seem surprising.

That the form of the garden would have been seen as 'Mughal' at the time we can scarcely doubt, as the symbolic significance of architectural style was by no means an alien concept in India at this time. The Mughals themselves had adopted distinctively Central Asian forms in key monuments (such as Humayun's tomb in Delhi and the Buland Darwaza in Fatehpur Sikri, both built during the reign of Akbar) in order to declare the dynastic association of which they were most proud, namely their descent from Timur. And they had refashioned the Persian *char-bagh* into something uniquely their own by combining it with funerary architecture, in numerous successive and enormous projects including the tombs of Humayun, Akbar and Jahangir and the Taj Mahal, each of which is intimately associated with the ruling dynasty. Given that in so many other respects (some of which will be explored below) Sawai Jai Singh's palace asserts Indic and *shastric* norms, this intrusion of Mughal court culture in the temple garden might be thought anomalous. It is true that Mughal garden plans had been taken up and imitated in Rajput courts before – including at Amber – but never before on this scale. A possible explanation is that the use of the *char-bagh* here was intended as a deliberate appropriation of Mughal imperial imagery: the application to '*Thakurji*' and his '*diwan*' of a form that was previously associated with the most powerful of the Mughal emperors. Interpreted as such, the garden plan would be entirely consistent with its patron's wider desire to emulate the authority of the outgoing (or so he hoped) central power.

The Naqqar Khana, with Udai Pol and the top of the Chandra Mahal visible in the background; photograph by Lala Deen Dayal

The Palace Plan

Our account of the buildings within the palace complex has begun with the temple and its garden because of the chronological primacy of Jai Niwas and the symbolic importance of the placement of Govind Dev at the centre of the scheme. To get a wider sense of the original palace layout and its derivation from *shastric* norms we need to broaden the focus and consider the plan.

At first sight the plan as it exists today is a jumble of courtyards of differing sizes: each is no doubt rectilinear in itself, but – apart from the boundary wall and the lines of shops that enclose them and separate the palace area from the thoroughfares of the city – they seem to lack overall coherence. However, at the core of this mass of building lies a sequence of seven courtyards and gates (in adherence to a *shastric* norm), and if we follow the sequence correctly, the original programme of the palace plan is revealed.

We must begin at the middle of the eastern side, at the Sireh Deodhi Darwaza, the great pink-washed gate on the public bazaar. 'Sireh' is a corruption of '*sarahad*', meaning 'boundary', so this is the principal 'boundary entrance gate', situated on the east in honour of the royal ancestor Surya. It gives access to a courtyard which various demolitions and accretions over the years have made scarcely discernible as such; the sole surviving feature of any age is the Indra Viman store in the north-east corner, a gigantic garage built to house a multi-storey chariot that was used in processions.

On the west side, aligned with the Sireh Deodhi Darwaza, is the second gate, the Naqqar Khana, or drum house, the upper part of which contains a gallery from where musicians announced the arrivals and departures of the maharaja with the piercing sound of drums and *shehnai*. This second gate gives access to a huge enclosure known as Jaleb Chowk. The name is something of a riddle. Local folk etymology connects it with the fried sweets called '*jalebi*', but this is almost certainly fanciful. It is more likely to be derived from the now obsolete word '*jalebdar*', meaning 'groom', indicating the court's original function as the stables and accommodation for the palace guard. In the early nineteenth century Victor Jacquemont observed that the soldiers of the guard pitched their tents within the courtyard, a space now cluttered with small buildings, tea stalls and the like. Soon after this, the function was changed as the ranges surrounding the courtyard were rebuilt to accommodate offices for the palace's administrative departments. The upper storey was added in the 1880s.

On the west side of Jaleb Chowk, continuing the alignment of the first two gates, is the impressive and ornamental Udai Pol, the entrance to the palace proper, named in honour of the rising sun. These first three gates were largely ceremonial: though they are equipped with strong wooden doors, the open spaces in front of them left them vulnerable to attack. But clustered close inside the Udai Pol, are two more, which are supernumerary to the formal seven and have a more defensive purpose: they break the axial alignment and are designed to channel any invading force into a couple of tight dog-leg turns. Appropriately they bear the more war-like names, Vijay Pol and Jai Pol.

Facing page:
Sketch plan of the
City Palace grounds

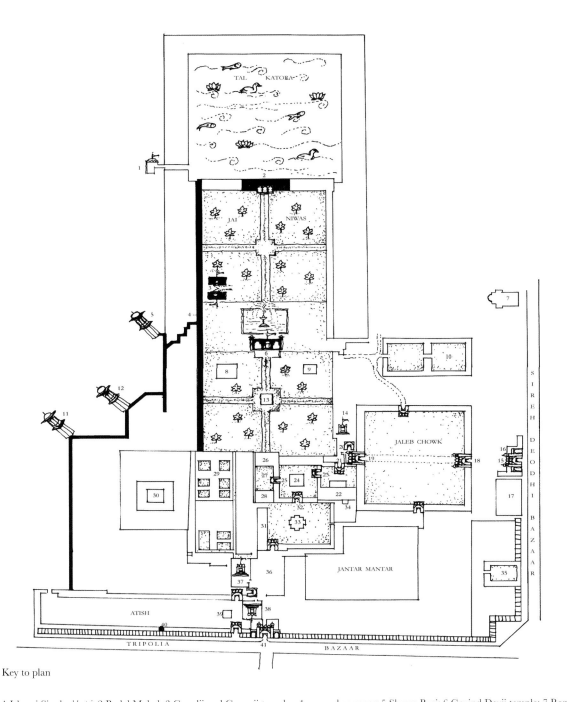

Key to plan

1 Ishvari Singh *chhatri*; 2 Badal Mahal; 3 Gopalji and Gangaji temples; 4 covered passages; 5 Shyam Burj; 6 Govind Devji temple; 7 Ram Prakash theatre; 8 Banquet Hall; 9 Kamal Burj; 10 Baggi Khana; 11 Chini Burj; 12 Moti Burj; 13 Jai Niwas garden; 14 Sitaram Dwara; 15 Sireh Deodhi Darwaza; 16 Indra Viman store; 17 Naya Mahal (Town Hall); 18 Naqqar Khana; 19 Udai Pol; 20 Vijay Pol; 21 Jai Pol; 22 Sabha Niwas (Diwan Khana); 23 Amba Pol; 24 Sarvato Bhadra; 25 Riddhi-Siddhi Pol; 26 Chandra Mahal; 27 Pritam Niwas Chowk; 28 Anand Mandir; 29 Zanana Mahal; 30 Zanana Majlis; 31 Bhawani Singh gallery; 32 Rajendra Pol; 33 Mubarak Mahal; 34 clock tower; 35 Hawa Mahal; 36 Chandni Chowk; 37 Brajnidhi temple; 38 Sri Pratapeshwar temple; 39 Baradari; 40 Isar Lat; 41 Tripolia

These defensive gates – for those who were privileged to be allowed through them – gave access to the third courtyard, which contains the Sabha Niwas, or Diwan Khana, the hall of public audience. Intended for the holding of *darbars* with the *thakurs*, and for the reception of visiting dignitaries, this hall is situated here in order to restrict access to the more private areas of the palace that lie beyond. On limited occasions, some of these people would be permitted to continue their progress westwards, through the next formal gateway, the Amba Pol, into the courtyard of the private audience hall, known as the Sarvato Bhadra. This was where the maharaja met his ministers and advisers in private conclave, and celebrated some specified events in the ritual calendar.

From this point onwards, access was very much more restricted as we enter the maharaja's private domain. To the west of the Sarvato Bhadra, the Riddhi-Siddhi Pol (sometimes called Ganesh Pol) leads via a covered passage into the Pritam Niwas Chowk, the courtyard in front of the seven-storeyed Chandra Mahal, the maharaja's main residence.

Even today this fifth courtyard is as far as the visitor is allowed to penetrate. But the sequence has not concluded. One of the painted gateways on the west side of the Pritam Niwas Chowk leads through a corridor to the sixth: the main courtyard of the *zanana mahal*, or women's quarters. To judge from their style, many of the buildings of the very extensive *zanana* were substantially reconstructed during the late 19th and early 20th centuries (in the reigns of Maharajas Ram Singh II and Madho Singh II) and the former plan is no longer discernible. But the original seventh and final courtyard of the series, a large open space containing a domed *zanana majlis*, or women's audience hall, is still extant.

In *shastric* literature, a maharaja's palace is conceived as a series of seven concentric enclosures: courtyards within courtyards, each entered through a ceremonial gate, and each helping to protect the innermost area, the *antahpura*, at its heart. The plan of the core parts of the Jaipur City Palace adapt this idea to a sequence of courtyards laid out in a row (an arrangement that is more economical and efficient, since more space is enclosed for the same amount of protective wall). But the paradigmatic number seven is retained; and so too is the key idea of increasing privacy as one penetrates further in. The sequence here is from east to west: from the public highway, through the court of the palace guard, through the semi-public and official courts of the audience halls and the private domain of the maharaja, to the furthest and most secluded courts of the *zanana*. And the sense

The Tripolia

42

that these innermost parts are protected by courts and gates in all four directions is enhanced by the additional areas of the palace that flank the central axial core on all sides.

Turning first to the southern portion, we may start our progress once again at a great gateway on the public highway, this time the Tripolia. Jacquemont tells us that only the *thakurs* and Brahmins were permitted to enter by the eastern gate, the Sireh Deodhi Darwaza, while ordinary citizens, including merchants and bankers, if they had business in the palace, had to use this southern gate. It leads first into an open courtyard known as Chandni Chowk. The name is not necessarily a reference to the famous thoroughfare in Mughal Delhi since the term '*chandni*' was in common usage in Rajasthan (literally meaning 'moonlit', a *chandni* is usually a terrace, in a palace or house, such as might be used for sleeping on in the hot weather). This one is surrounded by temples. In the south-west corner is the Sri Pratapeshwar Mandir, built by Maharaja Sawai Pratap Singh in 1794, containing a remarkable anthropomorphic *murti* of Shiva, in family conversation with Parvati, Kartikkeya and Ganesh. Ahead of it on the west side is the Brajnidhi (Krishna) temple, built in the *haveli* style that is typical of 19th-century temples in Jaipur. And there were once further Krishna temples on the eastern side, thus altogether creating a highly charged sacred space on the palace's southern threshold.

From Chandni Chowk we may turn left, towards the Atish, or royal stables; or right, towards the Jantar Mantar, Sawai Jai Singh's great observatory; or we may proceed straight ahead, further towards the palace core, through another gate into another outer courtyard. This courtyard was fully developed as late as 1900, when the court architect of the time, Lala Chiman Lal, constructed the elegant Mubarak Mahal in its centre, and inserted the Rajendra Pol in the northern wall separating the court from that of the Sarvato Bhadra. The Mubarak Mahal was first intended as a place to receive foreign visitors (Madho Singh II being even more reluctant than some of his predecessors to allow them into the palace proper); but it was soon converted into offices and now serves as part of the palace museum. The Rajendra Pol complements it in style and opened up a southern axial entrance to the private audience hall. The latest addition to this revamped outer court is the Bhawani Singh gallery on its western side.

Turning next to the area to the north of the palace's main courtyards, the dominant feature is of course Jai Niwas, the palace garden, with the Govind Dev temple at its centre, as already described. Access to the garden and the temple was obtained (by the maharaja) directly

Murtis in the Sri Pratapeshwar Mandir

The Kamal Burj

from the veranda of the Chandra Mahal and (by the common people worshipping at the temple) from a road that runs out of the north side of Jaleb Chowk.

An 18th-century court poet records that the garden contained fruit trees, including mango and lime, and flowering shrubs such as acacia and *champa*. But it also contains a number of buildings, showing that, apart from providing a setting for the temple, it was also a site of various courtly activities. The first of these additions chronologically is the Kamal Burj, situated in the plot to the south-east of the temple. The Kamal Burj, or 'lotus tower,' is a pleasure pavilion, a quadrangle of apartments enclosing a small water tank with an ornamental column in its centre. The date of its construction is not documented, but stylistically it can be assigned to the late 18th century. Balancing it on the west side of the garden is the Banquet Hall, containing two vast European-style rooms for reception and for dining. This too is undocumented, but in both style and function it can be assigned to the reign of Maharaja Ram Singh II, its construction reflecting the changed relations with the British authorities after 1857 and the consequent need to be equipped to offer hospitality in the European manner. Finally, to the north-west of the Govind Dev temple, are two small temples facing each other, dedicated to Gangaji (facing north) and Gopalji (facing south). Though designed in a traditional style, these are dated by inscription to 1914 A.D., and thus belong to the later part of the reign of Maharaja Madho Singh II.

At the far end of the garden, another pleasure pavilion, the Badal Mahal or 'cloud palace,' built by Maharaja Pratap Singh, overlooks the Tal Katora. This tank was the main reservoir for the palace, but it was also a place for relaxation: an 18th-century painting depicts Maharaja Madho Singh I boating on it. It seems that it could even on occasion be enjoyed by the royal women, as a passageway enclosed within the garden's western boundary wall leads from the Badal Mahal all the way back to the *zanana*.

This covered passage, and some offshoots from it, together create a strong impression of the potential for women to move about large parts of the palace complex in spite of the demands of *parda*. A warren of covered corridors formed their exterior world: it offered a temporary escape from the confines of the courtyards of the *zanana*, allowed them to oversee other parts of the palace, and even afforded glimpses of the world beyond the walls. Similar passages lead to the Chini Burj, the Moti Burj and the Shyam Burj, the three octagonal bastions situated on the western edge of the complex, overlooking the Chaugan or 'polo ground'. Of these three, the first two were for men only (the maharaja would be carried to them along the passages in a palanquin), but the Shyam Burj is fitted with *parda* screens and was intended for the exclusive use of the women. The Chaugan occupies the whole remaining area to the west, between the three bastions and the

The Mubarak Mahal

45

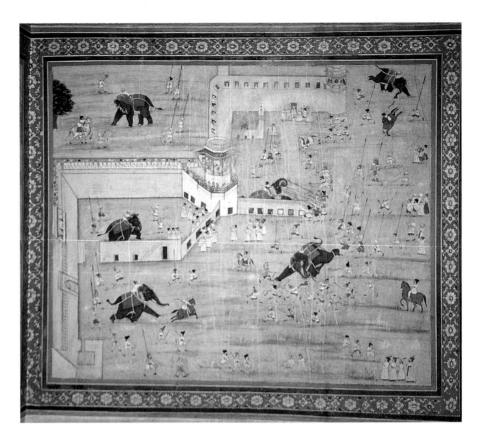

palace *sarahad*, and was used for more than its name implies. Elephant fights were staged
here, and the ground was (and remains) the end point for processions during certain
religious festivals.

Finally, to complete our survey of the plan, we need to turn again to the eastern
side of the complex where various additions were made, outside the central core. In
the south-east corner, at the end of the 18th century, Maharaja Pratap Singh added the
famous Hawa Mahal, a five-storeyed pleasure palace that has become the city's signature
tower. Although the patron's court poet calls the whole structure 'Hawa Mahal', tablet
inscriptions still in place suggest that the various storeys had individual names, such as
'Vichitra' ('wonderful') and 'Prakash ('light') Mandir'. What this palace chiefly provided
– that the Chandra Mahal did not – was a visible presence of the maharaja's residence on
a public street. Secluded within the innermost part of the complex, the Chandra Mahal
could not be seen and admired; while the Hawa Mahal served as a constant reminder to his
citizens of the maharaja's splendour and luxury. Indeed one 19th-century English visitor
at first mistook it for the main palace.

A later addition, to the north of Jaleb Chowk, is the double-courtyard Baggi Khana,
a garage for Western-style carriages that were acquired in the 19th century, and later for
motor cars. Slightly further north again, but with access from the public bazaar, is the

Ram Prakash Theatre, built by Maharaja Ram Singh II and used for both royal and public entertainment.

Palace Apartments

According to the *vastu shastras*, the palace of a Kshatriya king should be seven storeys high. The Chandra Mahal of the Jaipur Palace, comprising the maharaja's residential apartments, is the clearest example of this textual idea being carried into practice and is, in itself, sufficient evidence that its architects understood and sought to implement *vastu* principles. Most of the earlier Rajput palaces were built incrementally over many generations and any initial master-plan became obscured; while most of the later ones were more indebted to European ideas of planning. The Chandra Mahal is a rare (though not quite unique) example of a palace that was conceived and built in a single process, before European methods became predominant. In these conditions the traditional norms asserted themselves to the full.

The Chandra Mahal dominates the palace as a whole not only by its height but by its position. It is axially aligned with both the main entrances to the complex – the Sireh Deodhi Darwaza on the east and the Tripolia to the south – even though it cannot

Part of the façade of the Hawa Mahal

be approached directly from either; and it commands a view over (and from) the Govind Dev temple in the garden.

Preserved in the palace museum is an 18th-century drawing labelled '*tarah sat khan ki*', or 'plan of the seven levels'. Careful analysis reveals that this drawing is the architects' preliminary design drawing for the Chandra Mahal. In fact, only four levels are shown, but it is clear from some of the inscriptions and notes on the drawing that they are floors of a seven-storeyed structure (for example, part of the top-most level is labelled '*chandni sat khan ki*' – 'terrace of the seventh level'). It is possible that a section of the drawing, showing the lower floors, has become detached.

There are some discrepancies in detail between the plans as depicted and the building as constructed, but the basic conception corresponds: the rectangular mass of the main floors, the ramp (in place of a staircase) that rises through them on the western edge, the terrace extending on the south side (towards Pritam Niwas Chowk), and the series of set-backs on the northern or garden side – all these are plainly visible on the drawing. The discrepancies concern the internal disposition of some of the rooms. Evidently changes were made in

The Chabbi Niwas; detail of a dado (**above**)

the design at a later stage or even in the course of construction. What the inconsistencies suggest is that this is indeed a preliminary design drawing, made before construction began and not (like our own plans) a sketch made from the existing structure. This is also confirmed by some of the hand-written notes, which are in the future tense (such as the instruction '*gumbad bangaldar hosi*' – 'a dome and curved eave will be [here]').

Existing knowledge of the working methods of architects employed by the Rajput courts suggests that for most simple buildings plans were deemed unnecessary, as the approach was essentially formulaic. The '*tara sat khan ki*' is therefore an important document, as it shows that for a complex structure of seven integrated storeys, making a preliminary plan was indeed a part of the process. It also confirms that the Chandra Mahal was conceived as a seven-storeyed building from the outset. And finally it shows that even in this case the approach was partly formulaic, as some components are not drawn in detail but are merely indicated by words which describe well-established architectural forms, such as *tibari* (triple opening), *tibaro dhookyo* (enclosed veranda), *kotri gumbad* (square, domed room), *jharokha* (external balcony), *chandni* (terrace) and *bangaldar* (curved eave). All these are common components of Rajasthani design, and so, by merely naming them the architects

The courtyard of the Sarvato Bhadra; the Riddhi Siddhi Pol is to the left, with the top of the Chandra Mahal visible beyond could convey their intention to the builders. An architect wrote, 'This is to be a *kotri gumbad*', for example, and the builders knew what to do without further instruction.

The top-most storey of the Chandra Mahal, as it stands, is merely an open pavilion in the form of a *tibari*, known as the Mukut Mandir, to signal its function as the palace's crown. The court poet Krishnadatta Kavi attributes its construction to Maharaja Pratap Singh, so possibly the existing pavilion is a replacement of the original one.

Moving downwards, we come next to the first usable apartment, a suite known as the Sri Niwas ('exalted abode'). It is heavily ornamented with small pieces of mirror-work set in plaster, which is painted white and yellow (decoration that corresponds with some that was noted by Bishop Heber when he visited in 1825). On the walls are small paintings of flowers and vases.

Below this is the much more substantial Chabbi Niwas ('painted abode'), a large hall facing a broad terrace and flanked by domed rooms. The striking blue and white painting scheme was probably added in the 19th century, and it appears to be incomplete: some traces of superimposed drawing and pigment suggest an abandoned intention to add other colours, at least on the ceiling. The dados, however, are complete and may have been intended to imitate marble bas-relief carving.

The fourth floor has a similar arrangement and includes the Shobha

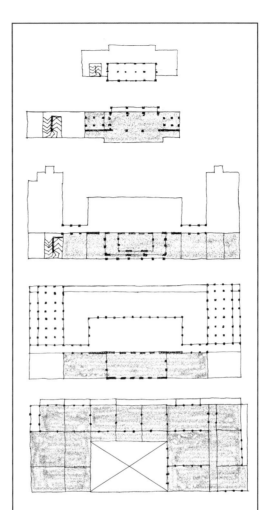

Left:
Chandra Mahal – plans of the five upper storeys. Shaded areas indicate enclosed rooms; other spaces are covered pavilions, open terraces and balconies. From the top: the Mukut Mandir; Sri Niwas; Chabbi Niwas; Shobha Niwas; and the apartments of the Rang Mahal surrounding the upper part of the Sukh Niwas.
Below:
The *'tarah sat khan ki'*; the original design plan for the Chandra Mahal

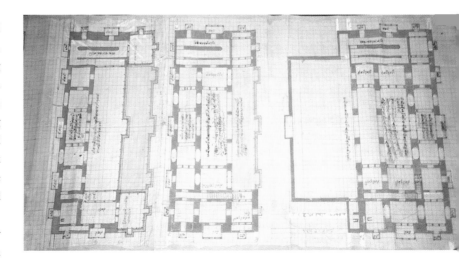

Niwas ('beautiful abode'), a throne room with red, green and amber glass and pieces of mirror and china embedded in gold plasterwork. The large rectangular mirrors with bevelled edges betray the 19th-century origin of this ornament, and indeed records preserved in the Palace museum show that this decoration was added in 1884. The third floor contains the Rang Niwas ('coloured abode'), a suite of rooms that was the maharaja's private quarters. Some fine silver repoussé work on the doors is amongst the surviving original features here; but the suite was refurnished in the mid-20th century for use by Maharaja Bhawani Singh.

The Rang Niwas does not occupy the whole of the third floor, but only its western, northern and eastern fringes. The large section on the southern side is a void, because the floor below is occupied by the double-height Sukh Niwas ('pleasure abode'). This

magnificent reception room is the grandest apartment
in the palace. Its doors open onto a large raised terrace
and, originally, the two spaces functioned together.
Krishnadatta Kavi describes Maharaja Pratap Singh
spending his evenings enthroned on a *gaddi* in the Sukh
Niwas, watching a nautch performed on the terrace.
The two spaces are now separated by a wrought-iron
veranda added in the 1880s. The walls and ceiling
of the Sukh Niwas were also repainted in a colour
scheme dominated by gold, between 1883 and 1885.
Some other rooms on the same level as the Sukh Niwas
(beneath the Rang Niwas) include a small *puja* room,
with fine, figurative 18th-century murals.

The main room in the centre of the ground floor of
the palace – the Pritam Niwas, or 'beloved abode' – may
sometimes have been used as an audience hall, but is
otherwise little more than a grand entrance. Beyond it,
to the north, there is a broad veranda overlooking the
garden. Maharaja Ram Singh II, who photographed it,
received even foreign visitors here. It is still used today
to house receptions for the Tazimi Sardars. The walls
and ceiling were painted, in imitation of carpet designs,
around 1900, and the portraits of various Kachchwaha
maharajas, by the Indo-German artist A.H. Müller, were
added during the reign of Maharaja Man Singh II.

Immediately in front of the Pritam Niwas, on
the south side, is the chowk of the same name, the
courtyard from where the palace is entered. This space
is embellished with four small but highly ornamented
portals. Tourist literature nowadays insists that these
gateways symbolize the four seasons (implausibly, since
there are six, not four, seasons in the Indian calendar). Their true significance is indicated
by the small *murtis* installed over the lintels. On the north-west is Ganesh, the god of
thresholds, because this portal is the maharaja's entrance into the *zanana*. On the south-
west is an image of Shiv-Parvati, because the portal leads to a small Shiva temple. On the
north-east (the dominant direction in *shastric* planning) is Vishnu, the principal deity for
this Vaishnavite dynasty. Devi is often associated with the south-easterly direction, and her
murti is accordingly found there.

Along the south side of Pritam Niwas Chowk is a two-storeyed range known as Anand
Mandir ('hall of bliss'). The upper part is now a museum gallery and holds a display of
arms and armour; though the original *sileh khana* (armoury) would have been a more

The Egyptian
room, in the Anand
Mandir

Facing page left:
The south front
of the Chandra
Mahal, seen from
the Pritam Niwas
Chowk

Details of the
painted *chajjas* of
the gates in the
Pritam Niwas
Chowk

Murtis on the gates
of the Pritam Niwas
Chowk: (**top left**)
Ganesh; (**top right**)
Vishnu; (**bottom
left**) Shiva and
Parvati; (**bottom
right**) Devi.

55

protected and secure apartment than this. The ground floor, perhaps originally intended for the palace guard, now contains offices. The maharaja's private office, now used by Bhawani Singh, is in the centre. The decoration, an Art-Deco rendering of the Egyptian style, was added by his father, Maharaja Man Singh II, in the late 1940s, following his involvement in the North Africa campaign during the Second World War.

It may perhaps seem surprising that in spite of building a substantial seven-storeyed palace it was necessary to have additional courtyards for the halls of audience; but this arose from the desire to separate the private from the official domains, within an overall zonal arrangement, as described. A surviving design drawing, similar in style to the *tarah sat khan ki* of the Chandra Mahal, makes clear that at least the closer of the two halls, the Sarvato Bhadra, was built at the same time as the earliest parts of the palace. The outer hall, the Diwan Khana, or Sabha Niwas, may have been added slightly later, after 1750.

They are both single-storeyed (though the Sarvato Bhadra has a small gazebo on its roof), with stout columns supporting foliate arches. Their similarity in form to the halls of audience in the Mughal palaces in Delhi and Agra has often been remarked on. The 19th-century travellers Reginald Heber and Victor Jacquemont both made the comparison, and they have been followed by more recent commentators. Clearly there is some truth in this idea and the halls reflect the founder's desire to emulate the splendour of the Mughal courts. But some further definition is necessary here if we wish to reflect accurately the cultural cross-currents of the period. To regard the Jaipur palace (or any other Rajput court) merely as a regional imitation of Mughal imperial culture, itself derived from Timurid and Persian sources, would grossly simplify matters. We have interpreted the adoption of the *char-bagh* form for the palace garden as an appropriation of Mughal imagery; but the

The Sarvato Bhadra

case with the audience halls is slightly more complex. The 'influence' was not always one-way.

A columned hall for holding audiences was a long-established component of Rajput architecture: the 15th-century Sabha Niwas in the palace at Chittor, for example, anticipates any Mughal Diwan-i-Am in both form and function. The many audience halls that were built in both Mughal and Rajput palaces from the late 16th century onwards reflect the traffic of ideas in both directions, and the joint development of ideas. The cusped arches and *chajjas* that both employ extensively were not foreign forms, but older north Indian ones that have been refashioned. The Sarvato Bhadra in Jaipur is especially distinctive. It derives its name not from its use but from its architectural typology: a *sarvato bhadra* in *shastric* literature being any single-storeyed hall that is open on all four sides but enclosed at the corners. It thus represents an indigenous reworking of the common idea, a combination of traditional conception and contemporary expression.

There is a more general point to be made here. Rajput and Mughal architecture display many common features and motifs, amounting to a shared vocabulary. Again, this should be seen as a sign not of a dominant imperial culture imposing its style on others, but of the constant interaction between the various Indian courts. Indeed, their shared vocabulary became in course of time a sort of generic north Indian style (even spreading as far south as Mysore, under the patronage of Tipu Sultan). But, in spite of this common vocabulary, the conceptualization of buildings often remained very distinct. This accounts for the Jaipur City Palace bearing so many superficial resemblances to the palaces of Delhi and Agra whilst being at the same time, in its plan and conception, the most successful expression of *shastric* ideals.

By the time the Mubarak Mahal was added in the outer courtyard in 1900, an entirely different imperial authority dominated the subcontinent. Although the political relations that the Rajput states established with the British Raj were in many ways comparable with

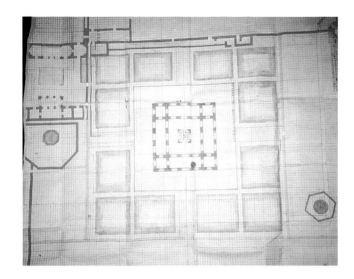

Top:
An 18th-century plan of the Sarvato Bhadra;
Bottom:
Detail of plaster decoration in the gazebo over the Sarvato Bhadra

Top left:
The Palace clock
tower; photograph
by Maharaja Ram
Singh

Top right:
The north front
of the Chandra
Mahal, seen from
the palace garden;
photograph by
Colin Murray for
Bourne & Shepherd

their earlier relations with the Mughals, in cultural matters things were somewhat different. In the first place, whilst fashioning their own imperial culture, the British were usually (though not always) rather less receptive to cultural ideas flowing from the Indian courts than the Mughals had been. The Rajput courts, for their part, were as receptive as ever; and so European ideas and styles came to permeate many aspects of court culture, but especially male dress, interior furnishing and architecture. One early sign of this in Jaipur was the installation of a clock in a pre-existing tower behind the Sabha Niwas. Intended to introduce a little Victorian efficiency and punctuality into court proceedings, the clock was supplied by Black and Murray & Co. of Calcutta at a cost of Rs 6,000 in 1873.

Even in the British period, though, the imperial influence was neither overwhelming nor unmitigated. The Mubarak Mahal itself, for example, though originally intended for the entertainment of foreign guests, is in many ways a traditional building. It is, in fact, another *sarvato bhadra* in form: the room in the centre of each side is open (through its veranda), while the corner rooms are closed; and the whole is planned on a *shastric mandala*. The architect, Chiman Lal, had trained in the office of the state's executive engineer, Samuel Swinton Jacob, an officer of the British PWD who was seconded to Jaipur for almost the whole of his career. Jacob had a considerable impact on architectural practice both in Jaipur and in other parts of Rajasthan, but as the Mubarak Mahal demonstrates, he had not come to teach Western styles: his chief passion lay in the revival of local traditions of ornamental stone-carving.

The Rajendra Pol, the gate that faces the Mubarak Mahal to the north, was built at the same time to complement it and connect it with the rest of the palace. Here too the carved and painted ornament is of the highest quality, showing how (in addition to Jacob's efforts) royal patronage had done much to ensure that the necessary skills continued to flourish. The sculpted pair of elephants standing in front of it was added after 1931, to commemorate the birth of Bhawani Singh, the first son born to a ruling maharaja since the birth of Ram Singh II, a hundred years before.

The addition of the elephants continued the process of embellishing the palace down to the present generation. But although that process was sustained over a long period and many generations, it will be apparent from the forgoing account that it was not smoothly continuous or uninterrupted. Rather, the building and elaboration of the palace proceeded by fits and starts. To begin with, the central core of courtyards and most of their buildings including the Chandra Mahal were constructed over a short period by the founder, Sawai Jai Singh II, in the late 1720s and early 1730s. His successors in the later 18th century made only a few, though conspicuous, additions including Ishvari Singh's Isar Lat (the minaret-like tower in the Atish court), the Sabha Niwas and Kamal Burj (probably both by Madho Singh I), and of course Pratap Singh's Hawa Mahal, Badal Mahal and Shiva temple.

No additions or alterations are documented as having been carried out during the first half of the 19th century, a period beset by political turmoil and regency rule. It was not until Ram Singh II came into his majority that building activity resumed. The major additions made by this ruler to the palace – the banquet hall, the clock tower and the theatre – in both purpose and style reflect his refashioning of the state in the light of developing relations with the British power. His successor, Madho Singh, turns out to have been the most prolific contributor to the palace buildings since the founder. Early in his reign Madho Singh redecorated much of the interior of the Chandra Mahal, ordered extensive additions to the *zanana mahal* (especially temples), and rebuilt Jaleb Chowk. Later, in the early years of the 20th century, he constructed the Mubarak Mahal and the Rajendra Pol and the two small temples in the palace garden.

Posterity has not been generous to Madho Singh's reputation. He has often been characterized as reactionary and cautious, if not idle. As he lay dying, a courtier who was asked to sum up his contribution to the state described him as 'a man who does not want to worry anyone and does not like to introduce new things. Whatever is established is allowed to go on.' The inaccuracy of this verdict (at least so far as architecture is concerned) is a reminder that even some courtiers had little access to the interior parts of the palace and little opportunity to judge developments there; but the comment also reflects a wider failure to recognize Madho Singh's role as a patron of palace architecture. His contribution ensured that the City Palace is a product not only of the vision of the founder but also, in almost equal measure, of the last great phase of Rajput palace design.

Detail of the
Rajendra Pol

FESTIVALS AND CEREMONIES

The celebration of festivals achieves an amplified state of pleasure through participation in themed activities that reflect the religious, social, political, and seasonal aspects of life in a given place. Food, dress, music and the rituals that are performed, work together to create a mood considered appropriate to the spirit of the occasion. Each year is divided into segments, marked by unique and distinctive festivals. Life in Jaipur and its former royal household is, till today, structured around these annual festive pauses, which allow its people to enjoy and reflect on the passage of time. Some of these – such as the spring festival of Holi, or Diwali in the autumn – are common to all India, while others, though not unique to Jaipur, are celebrated there in exceptional ways, such as Bhanu Saptami, Gangaur and Teej.

The City Palace has always played an important role in establishing, shaping, contributing to and sometimes sponsoring the cultural expression of festivals and ceremonies through song and dance, dress, customs and rituals, culinary and social codes. The City Palace is also the home of all the processional regalia that the people of Jaipur and neighbouring areas enjoy. For example, the *murti* of Parvati, who leads the procession on the two important festivals of Gangaur and Teej, resides in the *zanana mahal*, and all the cows, camels, horses and elephants, cannons, and military regalia that follow her through the city are also arranged by the City Palace. All this makes the celebrations a unique experience. If the role of the City Palace in the urban life of Jaipur is still so clearly visible

The Goddess is prepared for the Teej procession by Diya Kumari and companions in the *zanana*

Facing page: The Goddess's Teej *palki* is carried from the palace

today, even when the maharaja has no autocratic powers, one can imagine how strong the sense of royal participation in festivities would have been in the past.

One gets a glimpse of this from two historical sources that describe and prescribe these festivals and ceremonies of Jaipur. A complete list of such events including royal birthdays is included in *Pratap Prakash*, a court text composed for Maharaja Pratap Singh in the late 18th century. A much later work, officially called *The Ceremonial Procedure* but better known by its popular sobriquet 'Red Book', printed in the 1930s, again lists the festivals and ceremonies, and provides details about how they should be celebrated. Comparing these two works indicates both the striking continuity of ritual and conduct, and the gradual changes in festive programmes, which at a later date quite naturally incorporated new attractions such as cinema viewing as part of the celebrations.

What follows is a description of the major festivals that were and still are celebrated in the City Palace, having a significant impact on the celebrations in the city of Jaipur.

The year begins with Makar Sankranti, celebrated as the kite-flying festival throughout northern India. It is the only day that has a fixed date (14 January) in the solar calendar. As all other festivals are based on the lunar calendar, their dates in the solar calendar vary each year.

Vasant Panchami, the fifth day of the bright half (*shukla paksha*) of the month of Magh marks the advent of spring. A bright yellow colour (*basanti*) is adopted in dress to echo the yellow of the mustard fields. Women's veils and men's turbans (*odhnis* and *safas*) of a light pink colour are also favoured. *Pratap Prakash* mentions this festival and the sprinkling of *gulaal* (usually red colour) in the air in celebration. The day is also celebrated as Saraswati *puja* in honour of the goddess of learning. Marking the close of winter, the festival has a certain optimism to it, a renewed hope, expressed in the joyous songs on spring and beauty.

Bhanu Saptami, the festival of the Sun, is celebrated every year on the seventh day of the bright half of the month of Magh, two days after Vasant Panchami. It is an important festival for the entire city when the image of the Sun God descends from his temple in the Galta hills to visit Jaipur. The chariot of Shri Surya Narayanji arrives in Ramganj Chaupar, where he is received by the Household Officers and the *lawazma* (other functionaries). The deity then drives in procession through the Manak Chowk Chaupar and the Tripolia Bazaar, to arrive at the Amber Chaupar, where the *arti* is performed. The Maharaja offers the God a *poshak* (dress), one gold *mohar* (coin), and one *shriphal* (fruit). This festival dates back to the foundation of the city and is mentioned in *Pratap Prakash*. In the time of Maharaja Pratap Singh the procession included the Indradhwaj *rath*, a two-storey chariot pulled by elephants. This *rath* today rests in a building between Sireh Deodhi and the Dundubhi Pol (the door of the Naqqar Khana) in the outermost court of the palace complex.

Holi marks the culmination of spring. The festival is celebrated in two parts. On the full-moon night of the month of Phalgun, a bonfire called Holika Dahan is lit, followed by Dhulhadi the next day which is marked by playing with colour and feasting. People of

all ages and ranks lose themselves in greeting each other with colour, helped by mildly intoxicating delicacies made from *bhaang*. *Raag-rang* (music and colour), *gulaal-abir* (colours, usually red used in Holi), *mauj-masti* (delight and unrestrained joy), *gaana-naachna* (singing and dancing), and *peena-pilana* (drinking and serving drinks), are essential aspects of this festival.

Gangaur, falling on the third and the fourth day of the bright half of Chaitra, marks the beginning of summer, while Teej signals its end and the arrival of the monsoon in the month of Shravan. The silver idol of Parvati Mataji leads the procession through the city from the Zanana Deodhi on two consecutive days. The idol travels in a covered *palki* (palanquin) during Teej in the rainy season, and in an open one during Gangaur. The royal ceremonies are largely similar for both festivals. The Maharaja and the members of his personal staff proceed to the Moti Burj on the edge of the Chaugan (polo ground) to

Crowds in the city streets during Bhanu Saptami; photograph by Lala Deen Dayal

63

Maharaja Bhawani
Singh and
companions playing
Holi

Facing page, (from
the top):
The Palace elephant
is prepared for the
Teej procession;
the Teej procession
reaches the
former Chaugan;
the Maharaja
and Tazimi
Sardars watch the
procession from the
Moti Burj; (below)
Maharaja Madho
Singh I boating on
Talkatora; Jaipur
School, 18ᵗʰ century

receive her *darshan*. His Tazimi Sardars are seated on the lower balcony, while his guests watch the procession from the Chini Burj. On the first day the Maharaja and his staff wear a red *pag* or *safa*, and a green one on the second day. After the *darshan*, they return to the Jai Niwas gardens for drinks and refreshments. On the return of the Mataji to the Zanana Deodhi, *bhog* is offered and a *majlis* is held in the Zanana Raola (women's quarters).

In the late 18th century, the Gangaur procession commenced similarly from the Zanana Deodhi to reach the Chaugan, where lakhs of people received *darshan* of the goddess. Maharaja Pratap Singh sat in the Moti Burj with his attendants, all wearing the same style of dress. After the *darshan*, the Maharaja sat in a small boat in the Talkatora Sagar, amidst dance and festivities, and to a salute of guns and fireworks. The same programme was followed the next day. The dress for Gangaur was *gulambari* (yellow like the mango flower), *kasumal* (dark red) and *kesariya* (saffron). For Teej, all attendants wore *koch poshak* (a dress made of waxed cloth) and the next day, a *poshak* of *kasumal* (dark red cloth).

Gangaur is followed by the period known as Navratras. Maharaja Pratap Singh used to visit the Shila Devi temple in Amber and stay there for eight days. Hundreds of buffaloes and thousands of goats were sacrificed on the eighth day. Ramnavami, when the birth of Ram is celebrated in Galta, is on the ninth day of the Navratras. Teej is also followed by Navratras, which includes the Mahashtami Balidan, a sacrifice again performed on the eighth day in the Shila Devi temple in Amber. On the ninth day (*navami*) of the Navratras, a *puja* of nine horses is performed in the courtyard of the Sarvato Bhadra.

The tenth day is Dushera or Vijay Dashami when 21 guns are fired in the morning from Nahargarh fort, and a pandit performs the *pujan* of guns in Jaigarh fort. In the

64

afternoon, the Maharaja, dressed in a *kasumal safa*, *gulabi* (pink) *parcha achkan*, *churidar pyjama* and a sword, performs the *shastradi pujan* (worshipping of arms and weapons) in the veranda of the Chandra Mahal. This is followed by the *singhasan pujan* (worshipping the throne) inside the Chandra Mahal. The Maharaja returns to the veranda of the Chandra Mahal to receive greetings from his staff, officials, and businessmen (*seths*). The members of his personal staff accompany the Maharaja in a procession to the Diwan-i-Am, where he performs the *vahanadi pujan* (worship of vehicles) with one elephant, 10 horses, one *palki* (palanquin) and a *baggi* (carriage). On the appearance of the pole star (*tara darshan*), the Maharaja leaves the Diwan-i-Am for Jaleb Chowk, where a salute of 21 guns is fired. On his arrival at the Jai Pol, a blue jay (*nilkanth*) is set free. Next, the Maharaja arrives at Vijay Chowk and offers gifts at the temple of Sitaram, and performs the *kuldevi pujan* (worship of the deities of the clan) to Sitaram and Aparajita. *Prasad* and *dupattas* are presented by the *mahants*. The ceremony here ends with another salute of 21 guns. The Maharaja proceeds to an adjoining enclosure, where the Tazimi Sardars, their *kunwars* (heirs), and the Khas Chowki Sardars offer their greetings, followed by a *mahfil* (assembly and entertainment). After the *mahfil*, the Maharaja drives back to the City Palace gate, and then continues in procession on foot to the Chandra Mahal. A salute of 21 guns is again fired in Jaleb Chowk.

The programme as given above is taken from the 1930s 'Red Book', but Dushera has been celebrated in the City Palace with similar ceremonies at least since the time of Maharaja Pratap Singh. *Pratap Prakash* also describes the Maharaja performing the *balidaan* (sacrifice) to Shila Devi in Amber at the end of Navratras. On the ninth day, nine horses were worshipped, and on the tenth day (the day of Dushera) 10 horses were worshipped along with elephants and the 36 *karkhanas* (workshops). Lakhs of people used to gather to receive the *darshan* of the Maharaja during the procession which travelled one *kos* (two miles) to worship a *shami* tree (Prosopis cineraria) in the north-east corner of the city. The procession returned with torch bearers holding *dushankha mashaals* (torches with two flames). The next day, a *shalak* (gun) procession took place, and arrangements

Detail of tile-work

Facing page:
The Chini Burj

were made in Fateh Tiba (now Adarsh Nagar) for the lighting of all types of fireworks. Guns and cannons were fired from various parts of the fort, and their sound could be heard – it was claimed – to a distance of 12 *kos* (25 miles).

On Diwali, according to the 'Red Book', the Maharaja dresses in a *chundari safa*, a *saleti* (slate-grey) *parcha achkan* with a *churidar pyjama*, to perform Shri Maha Lakshmi *pujan* in the *kotri* (room) of Madho Niwas Mahal, private apartments attached to the Chandra Mahal. After the *pujan*, the Maharaja and the members of his personal staff proceed to the *chandni* (terrace) of the Shobha Niwas for a *mahfil*. The Tazimi Sardars, dressed in black for the occasion, are also invited. The fountains play and fireworks are displayed in the Jai Niwas garden while the *mahfil* is arranged. The places that are illuminated include Nahargarh, Ganesh Garh, the City Palace (especially the Shobha Niwas *chandni*), the Tripolia Gate, Isar Lat and the Rambagh Palace. *Pratap Prakash* describes the slopes of the hills surrounding the city being illuminated, and the whole city lit up with the light of Lakshmi. Lakhs of '*maunds*' of oil are consumed (a *maund* being a measure of weight roughly equal to 40 kg). The Maharaja surveys the scene from what the poet calls the 'Satkhana Mukut Mahal', the seventh storey or crowning pavilion of the palace.

The day after Diwali, the Margpalli ceremony is performed at the Karat Kot *darwaza* (the Kapad Dvar or private royal stores in the City Palace). For the Margpalli procession, a thick *bandanwar* (festoon) made of *kusha* and other grass is tied to the lintel of the main doors of the palace. The Maharaja mounted on a black horse is required to be the first person to exit under the *bandanwar*. The head of the horse is pulled back and the Maharaja extends his neck to be the first one to pass through. Sireh Deodhi is also known as the Bandanwar Door after this festival.

Janmashtami, Govardhan Lila and Annakuta, the three festivals celebrating the birth and life of Krishna, are centred round the royal household deity Govind Dev. The Govind Dev temple has been an important venue for these festivals ever since the foundation of the city, not only for the royal family, but for the entire population. Annakuta is a celebration of food, where countless numbers of sweets and dishes are prepared as an offering to Govind Dev and redistributed as *prasad* amongst his devotees.

As its name indicates, Sharad Purnima is a winter festival celebrated on a full-moon night. In the Textile Museum of the City Palace is displayed the royal dress worn by Maharaja Jagat Singh (r. 1803-19) on Sharad Purnima. It is made of fine white muslin.

Even today, the Maharaja and his personal staff wear a white dress with a pink *pagri*. The Maharaja lights an Akashi Deeya or lamp on the *chandni* (terrace) of the Chandra Mahal, and holds a *mahfil* on the lawns of Jai Niwas. They sit on white *chadars* (sheets).

Other festivals that are celebrated in the palace include Ganesh Chaturthi, where Ganpati *pujan* is performed; Jal Jhulani Ekadashi, where the idol of Shri Jasoda Nandji is taken to the Badal Mahal and placed in a *jhulna* or swing; and Dhol Panchami, where the *dhol* is worshipped amongst songs of praises of the late Maharajas of Jaipur. Shivratri or the festive night of Shiva has women carrying water pots on behalf of the Maharaj Kumar Sahibs and offering them to Mahadeoji Shri Panch Bakteshwarji located in the *zanana* garden. Such celebrations also include Sheetla Ashtami where Sheetla *pujan* is performed inside the Ganesh Pol in Amber, and in the individual *raolas* or apartments of the Zanana Sarkars; Nag Panchami, where *thals* (large salvers) of offerings are sent to Shri Hardeoji temple outside the Chand Pol gate; Mahalaya Shradh of Bara Shreeji, where offerings are sent to the royal *chhatris* at Gaitor; and Raksha Bandhan which involves an exchange of gifts amongst the family and important staff of the royal household.

Royal Birthdays

Royal birthdays and weddings are also included among the ceremonies described in *The Ceremonial Procedure*. Compiled by the Ceremonials Committee in the 1930s, today this 'Red Book' still retains a formal

status as a check-list against which the accuracy of the ceremonies may be judged. Whatever ever else one might do on the Maharaja's birthday, it must be ensured that all the rituals described in the 'Red Book' are performed to everyone's satisfaction (a daunting task), or else the organizing committee will never hear the end of criticism from all quarters, lamenting the loss of traditional values and recalling the glorious past when everything was perfect. According to the 'Red Book', His Highness's birthday starts with *gaja baja* (song and music):

> The officer in-charge of Zanana intimates auspicious day for the *gaja baja* ceremony. All *tazimi* and *khas chowki sardars* and the household officers are invited to assemble in the Sharbatobhadra to go collectively to the *chandni* of Madho Niwas. The *sardars* and the officers take their seats on *farash* of Madho Niwas. Naqqara Poojan is performed. *Paan biras* and *laung dodas* are distributed on behalf of the Zanana *sarkars* to all assembled. The *sardars* and the officers then return to the Sharbatobhadra.

In the above account, the central audience hall known as the Sarvato Bhadra functions as an assembly-point at the time of arrival and departure of the chiefs and officers of the household. The same pavilion, which is open on all four sides, has its *farsh* (floor) covered with a white *chaddar* (sheet) to serve as the meeting-point for the *gurus, sants* and *mahants* during the accession ceremony. The Maharaja proceeds from the Chandra Mahal to meet the officers and the *sardars* in the Diwan-i-Am where the *raj tilak* ceremony is performed, and then walks to the Sarvato Bhadra to receive blessings, *prasad* and a *dupatta* (ceremonial stole) from the assembled teachers and the learned. This open pavilion is a space which performs a role more private and intimate, both in terms of its size and function in comparison with the loftier Diwan-i-Am. It is physically also situated between the more public area of the Diwan-i-Am and the strictly private zone of the royal apartments of the Madho Niwas.

The 'Red Book' then lists the *daans* (ceremonial donations) to be performed on the birthday:

> On the Birthday, salute of 21 guns is fired from Jaigarh fort at sunrise. His Highness (dress: *chundri safa, parcha achkan* and white trousers, sword with red scabbard) performs 'Prayaschit Dan', 'Chhaya Dan', and 'Gao Dan' in the veranda of Chandra Mahal. HH goes to Sitaram Dwara in procession formed by the members of Personal Staff. HH performs Hawan Ki Purnahuti and offers *bhet* to *gurus*.

A *daan* is a charitable act that involves giving specific donations and is performed here along with a religious ceremony. A *prayaschit daan* is to seek atonement for any wrongdoings one may have committed, knowingly or unknowingly, in the previous year. In a *chhaya daan,*

the *yajman* or the performer, here the Maharaja, donates his reflection viewed in a salver filled with oil; and in *gao daan*, cows are donated to Brahmins. Next,

> HH and the members of his personal staff visit the following temples and *chhatris* to offer *bhets* and accept Dupatta Parshad from *sant, mahants* and *gurus*: 1. Shri. Sitaramji Bara, 2. Shri Sitaramji Chhota, 3. Shri Sita Ballabhji, 4. Shri Govind Devji, 5. Shri Ishwari Singhji Chhatri, 6. Shri Shila Mataji temple at Amber, 7. Shri Jamwa Mataji temple at Jamwa, Ramgarh.

This visit to the temples proceeds from those that stand within the palace precinct and ends in the Jamwa Mata temple in Ramgarh. For the accession ceremony, the list of temples to be visited, apart from the above, also includes the temples of Shri Rajrajeshwar, Shri Sitaballabhji, and Shri Gopalji, and the sequence in which they are visited is different. The full list of temples visited for *darshan* and the offerings made, is as follows:

1. Shri Govind Deoji	Rs.51/-
2. Shri Shila Mataji temple at Amber	Rs.51/-
3. Shri Jamwa Mataji temple at Ramgarh	Rs.51/-
4. Shri Rajrajeshwarji's temple	Rs.11/-
5. Shri Sitaramji Bara at Sitaram Dwara	Rs.11/-
6. Shri Sitaramji Chhota	Rs.11/-
7. Shri Sita Bhallabhji	Rs.11/-

Supervised by Maharaja Bhawani Singh and the *raj purohit*, Padmanabh performs the *chhaya dan*

8. Shri Gangaji	Rs.11/-
9. Shri Gopalji	Rs.11/-
10. Shri Ishwari Singhji Chhatri	Rs.11/-

Next on the birthday, HH performs the *varsh pujan* in the *kotri* of Madho Niwas followed by a concluding ritual called *pata uthapan*, performed by Her Highness after the Maharaja has departed.

The members of the Personal Staff, Household Officers and staff, and other important citizens offer their greetings to HH in the veranda of Chandra Mahal at a time convenient to HH. HH holds Zenana Majlis in the Madho Niwas and Zenana Sardars and other invitees offer greetings to HH. In the night, the Rajput Tazimi Sardars and Khas Chowki Sardars and the members of Personal Staff are invited to the Birthday Dinner or Drinks party at the City Palace.

So the ceremonial conduct progresses from the sacred formal realm and ends in the private or personal domain. Royal birthdays were celebrated by everyone in the city, and acquired the mood of a state festival through the participation of the people of Jaipur and of guests from other regions and nations. What the 'Red Book' does not tell us is how this participation was organized and facilitated. Clearly there is a whole dimension to birthday celebrations that is missing from the 'Red Book', and its exclusion suggests that some aspects were flexible and variable. Let us now look at two actual programmes of birthday celebrations in the 1930s.

Maharaja Man Singh II's Birthday in 1931 and 1932

The week from 7 to 14 September 1931, was celebrated as Birthday Week in the State of Jaipur, and a programme of events was printed for circulation amongst the guests. The celebrations started on Monday, 7 September with the semi-final matches of the hockey tournament, held in the Ram Niwas Gardens, followed by the first round of polo at the Jaipur Club at 5.30 p.m., and a cinema show at the Ram Prakash Theatre at 10 p.m. The next morning was devoted to the semi-final matches of the Squash tournament at the Jaipur Club and, at 2.30 p.m. in the afternoon, the guests were directed to the Chaugan to enjoy Village Sports. On Wednesday, 9 September, guests woke up to watch the semi-final matches of the football tournament, followed by the second round of the polo tournament. The next item on the programme was the *kul devi pujan* in the City Palace at 7.30 p.m.: the first non-recreational activity of the programme. The day ended with another cinema show at the Ram Prakash Theatre at 10 p.m.

Thursday, 10 September, was totally devoid of any sports activity. Solemnity and sanctity marked every item on the programme of this day, the anniversary of the actual birth of HH. The programme began with the review of the troops at 7 a.m.; and then

at 8.45 a.m., His Highness inspected the Jaipur State Boy Scouts outside the Rambagh Palace. *Varsh pujan* was performed at 9.30 a.m., followed by a Birthday Durbar in the Durbar Hall (Diwan-i-Am) of the City Palace. At 4.45 p.m., a procession made its way from Sireh Deodhi via Ajmer Gate to the Ram Niwas Gardens, watched by the guests from the top of the Atish (the stables courtyard) and the Public Library. In the evening, at 7.30 p.m., HH went in a procession from the Chandra Mahal to the Zanana Deodhi, where a *majlis* was held. The day ended with a state feast for the chief officers (*sardars*) in the Sarvato Bhadra at 8.30 p.m. That night, electrical illumination adorned the City Palace, the Rambagh Palace, the Albert Hall, the Tripolia, Moti Doongri, Isar Lat, Ganesh Pol, and the Deodhi Bada Raola (the main gate of the *zanana*).

The next day, Friday, 11, September, sports activities resumed with the earlier fervour intact. The whole day was devoted to matches. First at 7 a.m. was the final match of the football tournament with a prize-giving ceremony, and then the polo practice games at the Jaipur Club. The day ended at 8.45 p.m. with a state banquet at the electrically illumined Ram Bagh Palace. This enthusiasm for sports continued for the next three days with the

Maharaja Man Singh II enthroned in the Sarvato Bhadra on his silver jubilee, 1947

71

final hockey match, the Gymkhana races, pig sticking, the final squash tournament and the final match of the polo tournaments. The only non-sports activities were the cinema at the Ram Prakash Theatre at 10 p.m. on Saturday; dinner with the *sardars* in the Albert Hall on Sunday; and the polo dinner and cinema show on Monday.

The following year the birthday celebrations again lasted eight days, from Friday, 26 August, to Saturday, 3 September, 1932. There were the usual tournament matches of squash, polo, cricket, hockey, football and the Gymkhana sports. The day central to the celebrations, the birthday itself, as before, was a solemn and dignified affair, dominated by the religious rituals, processions, the *darbar* and the *zanana majlis*. The programme was almost identical to the previous year's, but differed in one respect. On six (rather than four) of the eight days, the guests were invited to a cinema show. On the first Friday evening at 9.30 p.m., a 'talky vernacular film' was screened; on Saturday, a 'vernacular film' exclusively for ladies was screened at 6.30 p.m.; on Sunday at 9.30 p.m. an 'English talky film' was shown; on Tuesday an English talky was shown to the ladies; on Wednesday and Friday at 6.30 p.m., there was a talky film, again only for ladies, followed by a cabaret show at the Albert Hall at 9.30 p.m.; and on the final day there was a cabaret show only for ladies at the Albert Hall, and this coincided with an English talky (presumably for the men) at the Ram Prakash Theatre, at 9.30 p.m.

On comparing the ceremonial procedure outlined in the 'Red Book' with the actual programme of events, it is clear that participation in the ceremonial activity varied according to the nature of the event. Certain procedures (especially religious ones) were conducted only in the *zanana*, some were open only to special officers and staff, while others

Maharaja Man Singh II with *morchals* and *chauri* bearers, 1947

72

were open to the public at large. The 'Red Book' leaves enough room to accommodate events and ceremonies that the specific ruler may wish to include in his birthday celebrations. One might say that before the procedure was laid out in a printed form in the 1930s, even the religious ceremonies conducted would have been freer in their form, and that the 'book' has merely fossilized them. Although the day of the birth itself was always

The Tripolia
illuminated, 1947

73

devoted to religious and sacred rituals, what happened in the week around that day could be different from one year to the next.

1931 was the year when the young Maharaja Man Singh was invested with full ruling powers, so his birthday in that year was his first as a ruling monarch. He was 20. As he was already a keen polo player and a fine sportsman, it is only to be expected that his birthday celebrations should reflect his interest in enjoying and promoting sports in his state. But the events also reflect the 1930s modern trends in India. The ruling and the urban elite participated in competitive sports such as cricket, hockey, football, squash and polo; they enjoyed watching 'village sports' and occasionally went to the cinema. With the help of royal patronage, Indian cinema was now flourishing, as had theatre in the late 19th century. In 1878, Man Singh II's ancestor had established the Ram Prakash Theatre, where for the first time female roles had been played by courtesans rather than men (acting being a taboo amongst respectable women). The same theatre was now used for the private viewing of films on birthdays. All over India, theatres were being converted into cinema halls throughout the first half of the 20th century, following the first such conversion in Calcutta in 1907.

If 1931 was one of the most significant years of Man Singh's professional life, 1932 was a turning point in his personal life. Man Singh was first married in 1921, to Marudhar Kanwar, a sister of Maharaja Umaid Singh of Jodhpur. She was then 22 and he was 10. When he was 20, he married his first wife's niece, the attractive Kishore Kanwar, whom he lovingly called Jo. While his first wife was conservative and traditional in her outlook, his second wife was 'modern' and undertook the task of running the *zanana* and making all the necessary arrangements on festive occasions. During that year's birthday week (calculated according to the lunar calendar as falling on 26 August – 3 September), the women guests enjoyed a 'vernacular film' and an English Talky, screened exclusively for them at the Ram Prakash Theatre. Cabaret shows that were generally regarded as entertainment for male audiences only, were performed exclusively for women guests at 9.30 p.m. on the evening of 3 September 1932 at the Albert Hall. Given her 'modern' outlook, the lovely Jo must have played a key role in ensuring that the women guests at the birthday party had an enjoyable time, and the programme reflected that. The programme is also a reflection of changing times. The ceremonial conduct at all times incorporates the specific interests of the ruler, the prevalent fashion and the fruits of technological advancement. The latter included the electric illuminations that were 'on up to twelve midnight in the city and outside from the 26th August to 3rd September 1932 both days inclusive. On the 29th and 30th August 1932 they [were] on the whole night.'

The birthday programme of 1932 has a few items that are marked with an asterisk, such as the opening of the 'village industries exhibition' and the ladies-only cinema show, the Birthday Durbar and the procession. Attendance at these events was by invitation only. In the case of village sports, those invited could enjoy the event from 'reserved enclosures or blocks'. Arrangements were made for the guests of the Maharaja to go out sight-seeing, and special arrangements were also 'made at the Sanganer Chopar for HH's guests to watch the Birthday procession'. Events such as the Zanana Majlis, Kuldevi Pujan, Varsh Pujan and the visits to the temples and Chhatris – that is, all the ritual ceremonies that the Red Book describes – were conducted, albeit in public knowledge, entirely privately, and they remain so today.

Since the year 2000, the Birthday of the Maharaja has been celebrated by conferring awards on distinguished experts in various fields such as crafts, literature, medical science, sports, architecture and social work.

Weddings: Gifts and Food

Hosting a wedding ceremony of the daughter of a household is an undertaking that requires extraordinary organisational skills, close attention towards every requirement of the invited guests and supernatural powers in anticipating their every desire. Such occasions are a hotbed of family politics, where a small oversight on the part of the host can be for the disgruntled guest an opportunity to open a whole catalogue of complaints from the past, present and future. If the wedding is a royal one, and thus directly under the critical gaze of the general public too, the challenge factor of the occasion is greatly enhanced.

On 9 February 1943, the marriage of Bai Sahiba Chand Kumari (Man Singh II's sister) to Raja Bahadur Udai Pratap Singh of Katiary was solemnized at the Rambagh Palace, Jaipur. The Rajputana Photo Art Studio was instructed to take as many photographs as possible for a suitable album of the wedding festivities.

Included among the details that are specified in the working programme for the event is the list of the items that were sent to the groom before the wedding ceremony as his *siropao* (literally, head and feet: a wedding gift arranged on *thals* or large salvers, usually comprising items of clothing and jewellery). It included a turban cloth embellished with brocade (*zari ka safa*); two bolts of fine cloth (*parchha thans*); one brocaded waist band (*zari kamarband*); a pair of embroidered woollen shawls stitched together (*dushala*); two bolts of cloth for welcoming the guests (*thans agabani*); a turban ornament (*sirpech*); one necklace; Rs 50,001/- in cash; one 'special' garland; one 'special-ordinary' garland; one special *pan* (a betel leaf with condiments); two coconuts, one covered in gold and the other in silver foil; and seven betel nuts (*supari*), two of which were covered in gold foil and five in silver

Crowds in the streets of Jaipur welcome the return from Jodhpur of Maharaja Man Singh II, following his marriage in 1924

75

foil. In addition to this, there were other *thals* with the following items: five *thals* of *pan*; 20 of fresh fruit; 15 of dry fruit; five of *mishri* or candied sugar; 60 of sweets and *batasha* (a kind of sweet made of powdered sugar); and five of *malas* or garlands. About six *zari thal-posh* (brocaded covers for the salvers) were made in Jaipur, and the rest were of coloured muslin and were procured in Lucknow. Four silver *thals* were similarly from Jaipur, and the rest were ordinary trays that were made in Lucknow. The whole array of *thals* containing these gifts would have been carried through the streets in a procession, making it a colourful event for the public gaze.

A wedding ceremony, like a religious festival, is a feast for the senses, where food, dress, and music play a central role in the celebrations. Of the several rituals performed leading up to the main wedding ceremony, one is *chandrama ka daan* (offering to the moon). The items that are required for the ritual reflect the light of the moon. They are: one conch (*shankh*), 5¼ *tolas* of silver, 2¼ yards of white muslin, 5¼ *ser* of rice, 1¼ tolas of camphor, one pearl, 1¼ *ser* of ghee, one silver moon of 5¼ tolas of silver, Rs. 11/- for a bull, Rs. 5/- for *dakshina* (donation). The items used in the ritual are all white or silver in colour, and are offered in measures that end in a quarter (*sawai*) which is considered auspicious and a sign of growth and progress.

Much more was recorded about this wedding, or might be inferred by comparison with other royal weddings in Jaipur. But perhaps what gives the best sense of the degree of care and attention devoted to its detailed planning is the set of menus prepared for the guests. One B. Manmohan

A Marriage Procession; Jaipur School, 18th century

Dutt was put in charge of the catering arrangements, with the food being prepared by the Khasa Rasohra (special kitchens). A 'scale of supply of meals' was established where three classes of menu were laid out (see below).

The menu has three categories of morning tea, smokes, drinks, morning meal, evening tea and dinner, presenting a delicious spread of food items, arranged according to the status of the guest (this being assessed by criteria that included wealth or professional standing, royal positioning, and personal proximity to the Maharaja in terms of family relationship). The range of provisions reflects the fashion of the time and what was considered superior. For example, Turkish and Egyptian cigarettes are thought superior to Russian and Indian ones; Calcutta *paan* is offered to the First-class, while the Third-class has to settle for the less superior Madras *paan*; eggs and toast with morning tea is reserved

	First Class Guests	Second Class Guests	Third Class Guests
Morning Tea	Tea, Milk, Sugar Kalakand Chowki 2pc, Buttered Toast 1, Bananas 2, Orange 1, Eggs to order 2	Tea, Milk, Sugar, Kalakand chowki 2, Dana 6, Bananas 2	Tea and Naashta
Smokes	One tin Gold Flake cigarettes with one matchbox. Some Egyptian or Turkish cigarettes.	2 packets of De Luxe Tenor or equal quantity of De Reszke cigarettes with one matchbox	Two packets of Falaknuma or 'Golconda' Hyderabad made cigarettes
Drinks	Whiskey, Gin, Asa and soft drinks as required.	One pint of Amritsanjiwani or Orange country liquor. Soft drink according to demand	Two pints of Angur country liquor
Morning Meal	Shikar 2, Zarda or Pulao 1, Tarkari 2, Mithai 2, Achar 1, Murraba 1, Papad and Phulkas, Poori. Total 13 varieties. Paan:- Paan Calcutta or Mitha 15, Supari, Chuna, Kattha, Ilaichi, Zarda as required.	Shikar 2, Zarda or Pulao 1, Tarkari 2, Mithai 1, Papad 1, Phulka, Poori. Total 9 varieties Paan:- Paan Madras 12, Supari, Kattha, Chuna, Ilaichi, Zarda as required	Shikar 1, Khuska (rice) 1, Tarkari 1, Dal 1, Mithai 1, Phulka. Total varieties 6 Paan:- Paan Madras 10, Supari, Kattha, Chuna, Zarda as required
Evening Tea	Tea, Milk, Sugar, Kalakand chowki 1, Agra ka Petha 2 pcs, Dalmoth 1 chhattak, 2 small cakes	Tea, Milk, Sugar, kalakand chowki 1, Agra ka Petha 1, Dalmoth 1 chhattak, Dana 4	Tea, Milk, Sugar
Dinner	Same as morning meal	Same as morning meal	Same as morning meal

only for the elite guests, while the third class has an unspecified category of *naashta* (the first light meal of the day or a light snack).

Although the elite guest is offered food that is more generous in quantity, variety and quality than what is in store for the ordinary guests, to read the range simply as hierarchical would be a misjudgement of its purpose. All three are offered non-vegetarian dishes, here defined in characteristic Rajput fashion as '*shikar*', implying game that has been shot rather than, say, chicken. The distinctions in the menu are also partly about taste and habit. For example, the host assumes that a guest who enjoys a cup of cooked tea spiced with ginger and cardamom, would not relish an English-style cup of tea where the brew, milk and sugar are served separately.

In spite of that last distinction it would also be a mistake to regard the menu as opposing *deshi* with *videshi* items. The foreign products specified are exotica, incorporated into a distinctively local conception of luxury. As in so many other aspects of Jaipur's courtly culture, novelties from abroad are assimilated without disrupting the established order or style.

The marriage of Princess Prem Kumari, daughter of Man Singh II, to Maharaj Kumar of Baria in 1947: (**left**) the couple visit the Jamwa Mata temple in Ramgarh; (**right**) the bridegroom arrives at the Albert Hall on an elephant

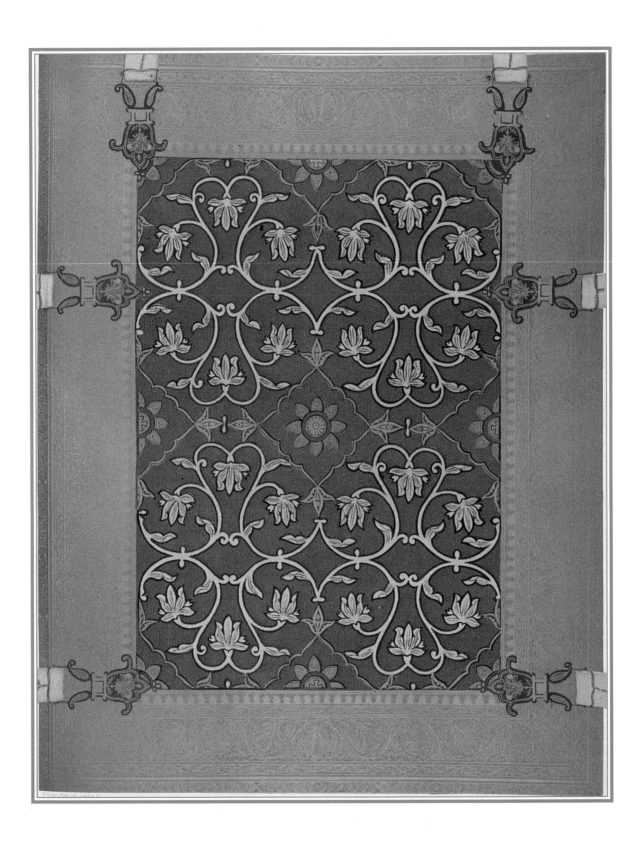

ARTISTIC IDENTITY

Pratap *Prakash*, a late 18th-century text on the life and court of Maharaja Pratap Singh, describes the setting of a public *darbar* in the grand audience hall known as the Sabha Niwas. The floor of the hall is covered with a seven-coloured durrie and a *chadar* (sheet) as white as moonlight, which is held down by diamond-studded *mirfarshs* (short bollards made of metal or stone, for holding down carpets and other floor furnishings). A silver canopy with an emerald fringe supported by diamond-encrusted columns and tied firmly with silken ropes, stretches over a velvet *gaddi* (mattress-throne) and *zarwafi takiya* (bolsters that are embroidered with gold thread). The sides of the Sabha Niwas are shaded by curtains and awnings. The maharaja wears a *mukut* (crown-like turban) with its ornaments like *turra* and *kalangi* (plumes) of pearls, a *kiran rumal* (cloth with a gold or silver lace fringe), a *jama* with gold embroidery, earrings and garlands of pearls and gems, a *partal* (belt) interlaced with gems, an *aliband* (a band to support a shield), and he carries a *dhoop* (a long sword) in his hand. His attendants carry a *gangajala jhari* (decorative container for Ganges water) and a golden *qalamdan* (pen and ink stand), while others bear shields, maces and royal fans.

All the objects mentioned in this description are products of artistic skills – in weaving, enamelling, armoury, stone and metalware, embroidery and jewellery – that received direct patronage from the Jaipur court and maintained a high standard of production in every reign. From the time of Sawai Jai Singh II, who initiated the plan of nurturing Jaipur as a centre of artistic excellence, every ruler of the state contributed to this founding vision. The art institutions that flourished throughout the history of Jaipur played a crucial role in the dissemination of manufacturing skills as well as in the production of objects. The Jaipur court supported these institutions through both grants and commissions.

For example, at the end of the 19th century, the School of Art was provided an annual maintenance grant of Rs 12,000 per year by the court. The School was intended to be unique in India. As the author of an early guidebook observed, 'unlike the School of Arts in the Presidency towns, the Durbar wished to make it more a School of Industrial Art than of the Fine Art; hence all those branches of Industry, for which Jaipur is particularly noted, received special attention at the time of the organization of the School.' Central to the success of this plan was the fact that whatever was produced in the workshops of Jaipur was immediately useable and consumed by locals and outsiders. The products were functional and decorative at the same time. New objects were continuously designed and brought onto the production line in keeping with changing requirements and tastes, so that fine enamelled cufflinks sat comfortably next to traditional enamelled bracelets with *makara* (crocodile) heads in shop windows.

Another important institution of the period was the city's museum, known as the Albert Hall (and still often called this, though it is now officially the Central Museum).

Facing page:
A breast plate from a suit of armour with *koft gari* (gold and silver inlay) work; chromolithograph, 1883

This was a place of public education and entertainment (and quite distinct from the museum within the palace, established later). The Albert Hall opened in 1887, following the enormous success of the Jaipur Exhibition of 1883, a display that projected local arts as standing at the helm of Indian design and productivity.

By the end of the 19th century, Jaipur was in a position to boast of an impressive list of industrial arts that had become inseparable from the identity of the city itself. The list included enamelware, jewellery, stone images, rugs, arms of all kinds, lacquered toys, semi-translucent porcelain, block printing and dyeing, brassware, book printing, papier-mâché, gold and silver lace, painting and photography. These skills and more continue to flourish in the streets of Jaipur, reflecting the vision and patronage of its past rulers. Even today, if one thinks at random of a list of ten artistic or craft skills associated with India, the chances are that the majority are practised and still flourish in Jaipur. The following is a profile of the portfolio of Jaipur's artistic skills, which reached their prime in the late 19th century.

Enamelling

Jaipur excelled in enamelling on gold, while enamelling on silver, brass and copper also thrived in the margins. Enamelling on pure gold produces the most satisfying result: a brilliant translucent colour that spreads evenly and thinly on the surface, providing a

Sword hilts
(**top left**) and a
cup, saucer and
spoon (**top right**)
ornamented with
Jaipur enamelling

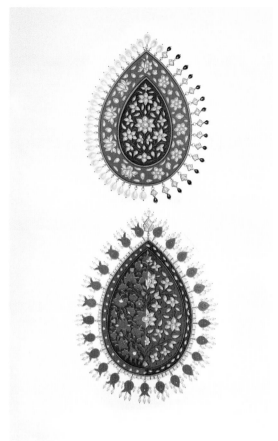

smooth finish. In the 19th century, Jaipur enamel had an international reputation for high quality as 'it is strong and doesn't crack and fly off as in many European examples of the art' (in the words of the Indian crafts enthusiast of the time, T.H. Hendley). A well enamelled surface is also an indicator of the purity of the gold, and enamelling was often used to protect this precious metal from loss due to rubbing against the skin of the wearer. This is why the backs of necklaces and the inner surfaces of bracelets, though usually unseen, were often intricately enamelled. Enamelling also provides a silky smooth surface to wear next to the skin.

There are two ways of securing enamel over a metal surface. *Champlévé* is a technique where the metal plate is dug out in shapes according to the design in order to hold the mixture; *cloisonné* is where partitions are created using wires to separate one colour basin from the next.

Different colours adhere to the surface at different temperatures. White requires the maximum temperature to set, followed by blue, black, yellow, pink, green and red. Red is the most 'fugitive' (meaning the most difficult to fix) and produces its best results only on gold. Jaipur excelled in ruby red enamel, 'noted for its fire and beauty of its red hues', and an enameller was judged (according to Hendley) by his 'power of producing a good pure red'. All colours can be applied on gold; black, green, blue, dark yellow, orange, and pink can be used on silver, and only white, black and pink are used on copper in Jaipur. First, a

An earring and two necklaces (**top left**) and epaulets (**top right**): *minakari* work illustrated in T.H. Hendley's *Jeypore Enamels* (1886)

83

chitera or an artist draws the pattern on the surface, then the *gharai* or an engraver or chaser digs the surface to hold pools of enamel; the *minakar* then applies and fires the colours in order of their hardness and, finally, the surface is polished with *kurand* or corundum.

Apart from purchasing ready-made enamelled objects from designated outlets, it was customary, even until the early 20th century, to commission enamelling on personal gold jewellery. One would take, for example, one's newly-made or purchased set of fine gold bracelets to an enameller to be covered in a design that suited one's taste and budget. For an ordinary ornament to be enamelled and set with gems, it would have taken three to four days for every *tola* of its weight. The cost for such a commission in the 1880s was between Rs 2 and 5 for every *tola* of gold. The design and production process entails a cooperative effort between the client and the designer, resulting in an object that has a unique and enduring design quality. Jaipur enamelling specializes in making small jewellery pieces, and even the large necklaces comprise small plaques that are treated individually. It was only around the turn of the century that large pieces like plates were attempted, mainly for the European market and for display in exhibitions.

Enamelling was brought to Amber by Maharaja Man Singh I in the 16th century, with the help of five Sikh enamellers from Lahore. The art was later consolidated for production and trade by Sawai Jai Singh II in Jaipur. After that, the Maharajas of Jaipur continued to have a personal role in promoting enamelled objects through gifts and commissions. For example, they presented the Queen Empress and other members of the British royal family with many large and valuable pieces, and these often found their way

A suit of armour with *koft gari* work, from the Jaipur Exhibition, 1883; photograph by Futcher & Stroud

Facing page: Brass plaques by Raghunath Khati on a door in the Albert Hall

into international exhibitions. The Jaipur enamels presented in 1876 by Maharaja Ram Singh II to the Prince of Wales later became a major attraction of the Indian Section of the South Kensington Museum. Maharaja Madho Singh II took with him modern pieces of Jaipur enamel as gifts during his visit to London on the occasion of the coronation of King Edward VII in 1902. He presented an enamelled cup and saucer to Queen Alexandra, who announced her appreciation by saying that she used it every day for her morning cup of coffee. The Maharaja presented a diamond-studded sword to his fellow royal, Edward VII, and was gratified to see that the King wore it on the occasion of the Indian army parade. This personal display of the Jaipur sword by the King Emperor would certainly have been noted with envy by other maharajas of the Indian States who were also present at the event. Placing these quintessential examples of Jaipur craftsmanship right at the heart of British imperialism was a shrewd political move by Madho Singh towards promoting the artistic identity of his state.

Many of the maharajas' personal items, like Ram Singh II's epaulets of enamelled gold studded with gems, were lent to the city museum for display. Perhaps most revealing of the court's support for this artistic skill was their patronage during times of general distress. It is during periods of famine and epidemics that the arts suffer most, but (as Hendley recorded) it was 'simply owing to the liberal patronage of the Jeypore princes, especially at times of unusual distress or scarcity of money amongst ordinary purchasers, that the enamellers, like so many more art workmen, have been able for a long period to remain at their capital'.

Metalware

Polished, it shines like gold. *Pital* (its local name refers to its yellow colour) or brass was being used for a variety of purposes in 19th-century Jaipur. Pots and pans, salvers, shields, boxes, trays, table-tops and doors were some of the items made of this strong and malleable alloy that gained popularity. Items used for consumption and cooking of food have to be plated in silver (or for a cheaper variety in tin) because the metal alloy reacts badly with astringent

ingredients. Silver-plated cutlery gained popularity as it offered the appearance and weight of silver at the price of brass. The difficulty with usable items in silver-plated brass is that the polish wears off and has to be regularly renewed. This gave birth to the specialist profession of *kalaigar* or tin-smith. Even today in the streets of Jaipur one can spot a *kalaigar* in front of brass shops, to whom the newly bought items are taken for polishing.

In the 1950s, just before the wave of low-maintenance chrome-plated steel that almost obliterated the use of brass in the cities, the following range of items were being used in the kitchens of India: *thali*, *taslaa* and *parat* (types of trays for different functions), *kalchhal* (ladle or large spoon), *chhalni* (sieve), *hauda* (large vessel for holding water), *jhara* (large perforated spoon), *sansi* (small tongs), *dol* (small water bucket), *aftaba* or *chilamchi* (basin), *silafchi*, *pikdan*, or *ugaldan* (spittoon), *husndan* or *khasdan* (vanity box or treasury box), *pandan* (betel leaf and condiment box), and *chiragdan* (lamp-stand). Within the religious domain too, brass was popular for utensils for temple rituals. *Aarti* (lamp for puja), *dhupdani* (censer), *katori* (saucer), *dipdan* (box to hold material for *aarti*), and *singhasan* (seat for the idol) were some of the brass items that were used in temples.

Engraving and hammering are two ways the surface of brass may be treated. The repoussé technique that flourished in Jaipur utilizes both. To make a salver, for example, a sheet of brass is shaped in the form of a tray, then cleaned and coated with white chalk or paint. The design is drawn or etched on this layer. It is then hammered according to design to raise the surface in relief. It is later chased, engraved and polished.

Pierced brassware, which allowed for the circulation of air, was developed for boxes used for keeping perishable food and damp items like soap. It was also used for lamps and as decoration for doors. For example, one of the objects displayed in the Albert Hall or city museum was, as described by Hendley, a '*pan*-box of pierced brass, silver plated, with delicate flowers and birds, which are formed, in part, by the perforation and, in part, by the engravings. The maker was Raghunath of Jeypore. This kind of work was employed for *pan*-boxes, as the tracery allowed the *pan* or betel leaves to be exposed to the air, but it is now often used for soap boxes and even for larger articles, as for example the door of the Honorary Secretary's office in the Museum.'

Two fine examples of Jaipur cutwork brassware adorn Rajendra Pol in the palace. The door and the lamp for the gateway were commissioned by Madho Singh II and executed by the leading craftsmen of the time. Raghunath, mentioned above, was among the best craftsmen, and excelled in repoussé work. Ganga Baksh Khati, another of the leading brassware craftsmen of the period, executed shields with repoussé panels based on original designs from the *Razmnama*, the most famous Mughal manuscript in the Jaipur palace collection. These shields were made only for display, to illustrate the technical skill of the workmen of the time.

Such uses of historical sources raises questions about copying and originality. New designs and motifs were often generated by copying objects depicted in paintings, or patterns used in architecture. The 19th-century patron was much more at ease with copying designs than the later 20th-century artist who would regard

copying of any kind as a sign of a lack of originality and almost as sinful as
stealing. Besides Khati's shields, a water bottle was reproduced from a painting
in the *Razmnama*, a tray was based on an arabesque design from Humayun's tomb,
and the inspiration for a prize winning salver was the cenotaph of Sawai Jai Singh
II at Gaitor. The copying of objects was encouraged (and not feared) to such an
extent that visitors to the city museum, if they so desired, could place an order for any
special article to be copied. All they had to do was point out the selected object
to an attendant who would then send it to the School of Art to be copied. The School
of Art therefore became an important centre of production, complementing the roles of
the museum and the court in the displaying and commissioning of objects. The students
learnt useful skills like brasswork, silver repoussé work, *koft gari* (inlaying of gold and
silver on base metal), carpentry, carving in stone and wood, and pottery. But Hendley,
the museum's Honorary Secretary, did not permit craftsmen to borrow and copy any
'European forms', with the exception of some Russian censers, which were perhaps
considered sufficiently Eastern.

Textiles

In the palace collection, apart from examples of local produce, there are some fine
textiles imported by the royal household, that bear testimony to the leading centres of
textile production in Chanderi in central India, Dhaka in Bangladesh, Radhanagar in
West Bengal, and Sarangpur and Burhanpur in Maharashtra. There are also examples
of textiles from Punjab and Kashmir, besides some imported European specimens.
Spanning three centuries (from the 18th to the 20th), the exhibits include clothes worn
by royalty during special ceremonies, festivals and events; examples of woven, printed

Woodblock-
printed textile from
Sanganer

and embroidered fabrics; and architectural fabrics like awnings, carpets, floor coverings, mattresses and bolsters.

The story of Jaipur's textile industry starts in Amber, where archival records of the sale and manufacture of carpets and fabrics are found. With the development of Jaipur, the *chhattis karkhanas* (thirty-six workshops) set up in the time of Sawai Jai Singh II included the *rangakhana* or the dyeing unit, the *chhapakhana* or the printing unit, and the *siwankhana* or the stitching unit. The *toshakhana* was responsible for the daily maintenance of the clothes and textiles required by the royal household. Jai Singh II brought in the best *zari*-workers from Surat, printers from Gujarat, and craftsmen from Malwa, to contribute to the city's textile production.

Sanganer was already a minor centre of textile printing then, and reached its peak in the 19th century as a centre for chintz. It was also due to royal patronage and commissions that cotton fabrics from Sanganer gained a reputation for possessing purity of colour, durability and variety in design. The printing industry faced competition from brighter synthetic dyes and from European dealers who began producing machine-made imitations that were cheaper. Machines were even able to mimic the hand-made look by blurring the edges of the design. Aniline dyes became popular with buyers as they could be applied repeatedly on the same fabric according to fashion and occasion. Since there are specific dress codes for different festivals, ceremonies and seasons, it was a common practice to re-dye the same cloth rather than buying fabrics dyed in permanent colours and designs. Therefore the market willingly embraced the sale of imported aniline dyes, deeply affecting the local dyeing industry. By the end of the 19th century, machine printing had arrived in India. And by this time European design also began influencing local printing, as samples were brought back through travel and trade with England. Madho Singh II for example, brought back European printed cloth from his 1902 visit to England.

One of the remarkable weaving centres of cloth, carpets and durries that flourished under royal patronage was the so-called 'jail industry'. Carpets produced by the inmates of the Jaipur Jail were in demand not only in India but were also exported to Europe and America. Persian, Turkish and Central Asian designs were copied. Those in Bikaner wool cost Rs 12 to Rs 20 per square yard; cotton-pile carpets cost Rs 6 per square yard; and cotton durries cost Re $1^1/_2$ to Rs 7 per square yard. Tents were also manufactured on a small scale in the jail. In addition to the textiles, there was a productive printing press called the Jail Press – also maintained by the court – that produced books in English, Persian, Nagari types and lithographs.

Stone Carving

Jaipur's reputation as a leading centre of stone carving has spanned at least a couple of centuries. It has been a supplier of marble images of sacred deities and later of statues of political leaders all over India. These images were plain, coloured, or gilded. Images were also carved in black and red marble, and decorative carving was made in cream coloured

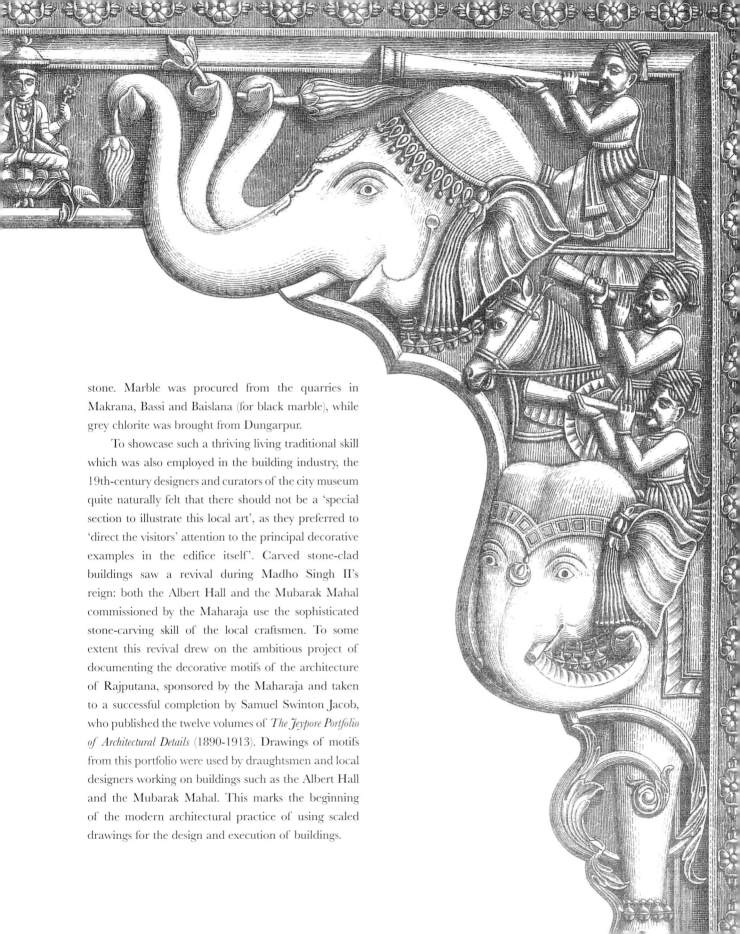

stone. Marble was procured from the quarries in Makrana, Bassi and Baislana (for black marble), while grey chlorite was brought from Dungarpur.

To showcase such a thriving living traditional skill which was also employed in the building industry, the 19th-century designers and curators of the city museum quite naturally felt that there should not be a 'special section to illustrate this local art', as they preferred to 'direct the visitors' attention to the principal decorative examples in the edifice itself'. Carved stone-clad buildings saw a revival during Madho Singh II's reign: both the Albert Hall and the Mubarak Mahal commissioned by the Maharaja use the sophisticated stone-carving skill of the local craftsmen. To some extent this revival drew on the ambitious project of documenting the decorative motifs of the architecture of Rajputana, sponsored by the Maharaja and taken to a successful completion by Samuel Swinton Jacob, who published the twelve volumes of *The Jeypore Portfolio of Architectural Details* (1890-1913). Drawings of motifs from this portfolio were used by draughtsmen and local designers working on buildings such as the Albert Hall and the Mubarak Mahal. This marks the beginning of the modern architectural practice of using scaled drawings for the design and execution of buildings.

Pottery

Numerous centres of pottery production had already made a mark by the late 19th century and were prominent enough to be represented in display cabinets in the city museum. Amongst these were Bulandshahr, Jalandhar, Peshawar, Bhawalpur, Multan, Hola (Sind), Patan, Bombay, Madras and Ceylon. Overseas specimens included Japanese and Hungarian examples, English porcelain such as Worcestershire and Doulton ware, and Turkish red and black pottery.

Jaipur had earlier been a home of white clay pottery which had been introduced from Delhi; but the city's distinctive blue painted pottery was consolidated as a craft form with the opening of the School of Art in 1866, where the technique was taught and practised. Yellow clay and feldspar are the main ingredients and both are available locally. Moulded pots and vessels are joined and coated with powdered white feldspar mixed with starch. They are then painted with an oxide of cobalt for blue, and oxide of copper for green. The painted item is then dipped in a glaze of glass, and baked when dry. New items and shapes of pots, vases, flasks, jars, cups, plates and bowls were introduced to rejuvenate the pottery market.

Detail of stone carving on the Mubarak Mahal in the City Palace

Some of the designs on the vessels that were exhibited in the museum were copied from painted decorations on the palace walls at Amber. Within a traditional system of artistic production, there is a natural sharing of design principles or concepts; but this deliberate crossover of historical patterns and motifs from architecture to artefacts in pottery and brass was something quite new, which led to the formation of a unified and recognizable identity of Jaipur's art. There is a distinction to be made between designs in different media that are generated by a single shared system or vocabulary, and patterns that are simply copied from one medium to another. So, for example, when a *jaali* motif is used variously in architecture, brassware and textiles, it is the working out of the concept in these different media that shapes the final – sometimes very different – products. By contrast, simply copying the design in different media will result in geometrically identical versions.

'Jaipur blue' pottery vases, displayed in the Jaipur Exhibition, 1883

Lacquer Work

Lacquer work in wood and lac-turnery are skills that flourished in the Punjab, Sind, Rajputana, and the North-western Provinces of 19th century India. Lac-turnery involves using a lathe to turn wood into round objects and covering them with variously coloured layers of shellac. The design is etched on the surface revealing different colours according to the depth of the etched line. Madho Singh II lent exquisite examples of Jaipur lacquer work to the city museum, including painted and lacquered staves and three maces covered with motifs. The Jaipur School of Art then produced vases, bottles and boxes decorated with animal and bird motifs copied from the maces.

Photography

The reigns of Maharajas Ram Singh II and Madho Singh II coincided with the emergence of a new and dominant mode of representation, namely photography. The medium was introduced into India in 1840s, immediately following its invention in Europe. It was soon recognized as a practically useful and visually arresting form of picture making, and from the 1860s it was enthusiastically taken up for both official and commercial purposes by Indian as well as British elites. It received special attention in Jaipur due to the personal interest of Maharaja Ram Singh and by the end of the century it was being used for a variety of purposes. The palace museum contains a large number of photographs, reflecting the role of the Jaipur court in collecting, commissioning and even producing photographic images.

The first figure who deserves mention in any account of photography in Jaipur is Maharaja Ram Singh himself, a gifted amateur photographer. This distinction is claimed for one or two others amongst Indian rulers, but the extent to which they engaged in photography as practitioners rather than as patrons and collectors has yet to be fully determined. In the case of Ram Singh things are quite clear: though his work was forgotten for many years, his engagement was put beyond doubt by the rediscovery in the mid-20th century of his cameras, lenses, glass plates and autographed albumen prints. It is known that between 1866 and 1880 he engaged a British professional photographer – one T. Murray based in Nainital – as his assistant or guide, but for the most part a clear distinction can be made between the works attributed to each that are now in the palace museum archives. The only exceptions to this rule are some that have been called 'self-portraits' of the maharaja, which logically must have involved an assistant.

Ram Singh came to the throne as an infant in 1835. The year of the Indian Rebellion, 1857, was a watershed in his reign as the years following that upheaval were marked by the greater stability of the Jaipur state and the increased personal authority of the now mature ruler. In the early part of his reign, developments in the political and cultural life of the city and the court had been the work of his regency council (led by the *rajmata*) or of British Residents such as John Ludlow, acting through him. The founding of the Maharaja's College in 1844, for example, was really the initiative of two of his early mentors, John Ludlow and Pandit Shiv Deen. But we may fairly assume that the causes and interests that Ram Singh espoused after 1857 were of his personal choosing. One of these was photography. It is believed that he acquired his first camera in 1862. It is quite clear that he had mastered the medium by 1866: in that year he was visited by the French traveller Louis Rousselet, himself a keen photographer, who mentions discussing the subject with Ram Singh and admiring his work. By the end of that decade (at the latest) he was a subscribing life member of the Bengal Photographic Society.

Ram Singh found most of his subjects close at hand. The great majority of his photographs are views of the palace or of buildings within the walled city, and portraits of the palace's inhabitants. Some of the portraits show eminent courtiers and advisers, while others depict *pardayats*, lowly members of the *zanana*. A proportion of the latter are reported on good authority to be nudes, but these are not currently accessible; the better known images show women clothed and so incidentally provide much information about court costume of the period.

Technically more accomplished was the work of India's most famous 19th-century photographer, Lala Deen Dayal (1844-1905). As is well known, Deen Dayal studied at Thomason Engineering College in Roorkee and then worked for

A *pardayat*
– a woman of the
zanana; photograph
by Maharaja Ram
Singh

the Public Works Department of Indore before he was appointed court photographer to the Nizam of Hyderabad in 1884. According to his own testimony, his early efforts were encouraged by the Agent to the Governor General for Central India, Sir Henry Daly, who arranged for him to photograph distinguished visitors to Indore including the Viceroy Lord Northbrook and, later, the Prince of Wales. The Prince's

Indian tour (1875-6) also included Jaipur, but although that visit was recorded by other photographers it seems likely that Deen Dayal first visited the city somewhat later.

It is also apparent that Maharaja Ram Singh at some point ordered from him a set of views of Amber and Jaipur, to be assembled in an album. Undertaken intermittently, or delayed by other commitments, the work was not fully accomplished until 1888. By this date Ram Singh had died (and was succeeded by Madho Singh), but Deen Dayal was still remembered in Jaipur: he had won the gold medal for photography in the Jaipur Exhibition of 1883. Eleven copies of his tardily delivered album of thirty views (some incomplete) now remain in the palace museum. This was not among the albums that were advertised by Deen Dayal's company for sale to the general public (being instead a private commission) but some of the individual images were also included in Deen Dayal's large commercial album, *Views of Rajputana*, and some were available separately. This explains their appearance in many other collections today.

There are also many imitations. As with so many other places, Deen Dayal's images of Amber and Jaipur set a standard which later photographers sought to emulate, selecting the same subjects and vantage points. His views of the palace and fort at Amber were especially successful in this regard. Even more evocative of the period are his views of views of the graceful temples at the pilgrimage site at Galta and of the

A dancing girl
with musicians;
photograph by
Maharaja Ram Singh
(see also page 58)

95

crowds celebrating the spring festival of Bhanu Saptami.

Much less well known outside Jaipur are Gobindram and Oodeyram, who ran the city's leading photographic studio at the turn of the century. They operated from premises in Chandpol Bazaar from the late 1880s. Some of their topographical views suggest the influence of Deen Dayal (whose work they could doubtless have seen in the royal collections). More original and arresting are their ethnographical images, of which they produced a large number. Projects of this type, especially those undertaken by British photographers, have understandably been associated with colonial authority and control over Indian society: works such as the multi-volume *People of India* series (1868-75) and William Johnson's *Oriental Races* (1863-66) seem to embody a distinctively colonial gaze. But the representation of castes also has roots in Company painting, undertaken by Indian artists earlier in the century (albeit mostly for Western consumption). Gobindram and Oodeyram's work shows the genre operating in a wholly Indian context. Some of their images – particularly those of dancing girls – were later reproduced as popular postcards.

Among the British photographers of this period who published images of Jaipur, the best known is the company of Bourne and Shepherd, which had studios in Simla, Calcutta and Bombay. Their images are numerous and widespread: as they could be purchased individually (rather than as sets) they turn up in mixed albums that were assembled by private collectors. Copies of them frequently occur also in albums that are attributed to Samuel Bourne, so it is worth noting that Bourne himself seems never to have visited Jaipur. The photographs of the city advertised in the company's catalogue were taken by Colin Murray in the winter of 1872-3. These works are well represented in the palace museum collection, having been acquired by Maharaja Ram Singh.

The Bourne and Shepherd images are architectural and scenic, and while they thus capture one important aspect of the city and palace, they overlook the industrial arts for which Jaipur was already just as famous. This lacuna was filled in 1883, at the time of the Jaipur Exhibition when Corporals Futcher and Stroud of the Royal Engineers were recruited from Roorkee to photograph all the exhibits (see page 84). Their images were included in Thomas Holbein Hendley's magnificent four-

Temples at Galta; photograph by Lala Deen Dayal (see also pages 8-9, 39, 63 and 135)

Preceding pages: The Hawa Mahal; photograph by Colin Murray for Bourne & Shepherd

volume retrospective catalogue, *Memorials of the Jeypore Exhibition*, published under the patronage of Maharaja Sawai Madho Singh II.

Those named above are merely the best known and most prolific of the photographers whose works are included in the palace museum. The large number of historic photographs in the collection – including over 140 albums – is a measure of the importance given to photography in court culture of the period. This is a subject which requires some further comment, particularly in the light of a common misconception. It is sometimes suggested that the introduction of photography spelt doom for traditional Indian court painting, that as the new medium took hold, the

older one, unable to compete, died out. We suggest that this view seriously misreads the historical record. It has to be conceded that superficially it seems supported by common sense: a particular style of courtly miniature painting that had flourished and developed in diverse regional schools from the mid-16th century onwards, by and large ceased by the mid-19th, and the appearance of India's later rulers is better known through photographs. But to suggest that the new medium replaced painting is a gross simplification. There was in fact a long period of creative interaction between the two media. Court artists of the late 19th and early 20th centuries used photography in a variety of ways: they began to base their compositions on photographs, or to adopt the pictorial formulae of photography, or to apply colour to actual photographs. To describe such responses as artists slavishly imitating photography is to evince a prejudice that undervalues their creativity. One might rather say that the artists assimilated the new technology into the continuing tradition of image-making.

This is particularly evident in the case of Jaipur, where there survive a large number of portraits inspired by known photographic models, and hand-coloured photographic prints, depicting Ram Singh II, Madho Singh II and even the young Man Singh II (the latter from as late as the 1920s). At the same time the court continued to offer patronage to painters, both local and foreign, up until the 1940s (one conspicuous example is the series of historical portraits of Jaipur's rulers commissioned by Man Singh II from the Indo-German artist A.H. Müller, that adorn the veranda of the Chandra Mahal). What put paid to Indian court painting was not the introduction of a new technology but the political demise of the courts themselves.

The lower pool at Galta; photograph by Colin Murray for Bourne & Shepherd (see also preceding pages, and pages 58 and 112)

In a similar way, we suggest that it would be wrong to regard photography, despite its origins, as specifically 'Western'. It was mastered by Indian practitioners within a few years of its invention, making its history in India as long as anywhere. Patrons in Indian courts, as they fashioned and projected their image for public consumption, selected those novelties that would serve their purpose. Thus Ram Singh II ordered gas lamp-posts for the streets of Jaipur not because they were 'European' but because they were modern and beneficial. From the perspective of an Indian maharaja, confident of his authority, modernity bore no foreign stamp. Photography was not imposed on Jaipur by the example of a dominant colonial power, but chosen by the ruler as a new instrument to project the always developing culture and identity of the Jaipur court.

It also played a role in public education, under the maharajas' patronage. Objects and artefacts from distant lands could be visually brought to Jaipur through photography. For example, photographs of the most famous objects in the great museum at Cairo were displayed in Jaipur's city museum. Photographs of the royal mummies found at Deir-el-Bahari, near Thebes in 1881, along with places of interest in Egypt accompanied them. In order to provide an insight into the variety and richness of the built heritage of India itself, photographs of important ancient buildings in Rajputana, Malwa, Bombay, Agra, Delhi and its neighbourhood were similarly displayed. Conversely, images of Jaipur and Rajputana travelled far and

Top (left and right): Jaipur dancing girls; postcards after photographs by Gobindram and Oodeyram

wide through exhibitions like those held in Lahore and Simla, where (according to Hendley) photographs taken by 'native artists' (meaning Indian professional photographers) showed 'views of the principal places of interest in the Jaipur State, and of famous buildings in Rajputana and Central India'.

This use of photographs in the city museum was intended to facilitate both education and dissemination. Again, according to Hendley, they were there not only for 'the visitor to study the art themselves very thoroughly, but, in most cases to have reproductions made of the finest examples, because Jaipur craftsmen can copy almost anything of an oriental character with great success.' Coloured photographs of buildings and places of interest in Jaipur were displayed, the colour being added on the black and white images to indicate the type of stone used.

Outside the confines of the museum was a flourishing trade in photographic prints. Gobindram and Oodeyram of Chandpol Bazaar sold both photographs and paintings. According to a Thomas Cook guidebook of 1899, one could buy 'native pictures' from Messrs. S. Zoraster & Co. on Motisingh Bhomia ka Rasta off Johari Bazar, Messrs. Gobindram and Oodeyram, Messrs. P.M. Alabuksh & Co. on Chaura Rasta, and from Kalu Ram on Johari Bazar. These shops were also dealers in handicrafts and textiles, showing the extent to which photography had become integrated with the wider field of Jaipur's visual culture and commerce.

'Sleeping Hindoo Woman'; photograph by Gobindram and Oodeyram

Royal Participation

Art and literature received active patronage, to a lesser or a greater degree in every reign. Apart from the general support to creative activities like painting, music, architecture and literature, some of the maharajas themselves exercised their creative skills. Sawai Jai Singh II was a keen enthusiast of astronomy, which translated itself into the building of observatories and his work on an almanac (discussed in the chapter on Education). The next significant period of Jaipur being led by a creative individual was the reign of Maharaja Pratap Singh, a poet, a musician and a *rasik* – a connoisseur of the arts. He wrote poetry under the sobriquet Vrajanidhi and nearly 30 works attributed to him have been identified. Among them are *Padmamuktavali*, *Phagaranga*, *Shringaramanjari* and *Premapanth*, titles which indicate the author's intellectual engagement with literary and aesthetic theory as much as with artistic practice. The main courtly text of his period, *Pratap Prakash* by Krishna Datta, describes him enjoying a game of chess on the candle-lit and incense-infused terrace of the Sukh Niwas, on the first floor of the Chandra Mahal in the City Palace. This is followed by a song and dance performance, accompanied by the following musical instruments: *mridanga*, *sitar*, *taar*, *krataar*, *veena*, *kinnar*, *kanoor*, *dayara*, *dukad*, *sarangi*, *bansi*, and *algoza*. Pratap Singh also practised the art of paper-cutting, and the palace museum holds intricate examples of his designs.

Ram Singh II too was an enlightened ruler, passionate about the promotion of the arts. He was an avid fan of modern visual media, including theatre as well as photography. He attended performances in theatres in Calcutta and, at home, he sponsored plays and musicals staged in his own purpose-built theatre, Ram Prakash. This theatre was later used for cinema viewing during Man Singh II's reign.

It was during Madho Singh II's reign that all the crafts and the arts were consolidated through his visionary patronage to establish the cohesive artistic identity of Jaipur. This was made possible by his support for exhibitions, his personal interest in the city museum and his initiative in lending personal items for display, his taking items that were products of Jaipur craftsmanship as gifts during royal events in India and abroad, and his commissioning of projects of documentation such as *The Jeypore Portfolio*. He was also the initiator of the hotel industry in Jaipur, as in 1882, the Darbar sanctioned the opening of the city's first purpose-built hotel, the Kaiser-i-Hind. The hotel was declared in 1899 by one of its clients, S. Rayner, to be 'very comfortable and clean. Cooking excellent. Stayed here ten days, and consider it one of the best hotels in India.' The Dak Bungalow was also converted into the Jaipur Hotel, and both hotels were managed under the supervision of the court. The Maharaja's intention in promoting tourism was to attract a broader audience and clientele for Jaipur's arts, thus initiating in its modern form a phenomenon that continues today.

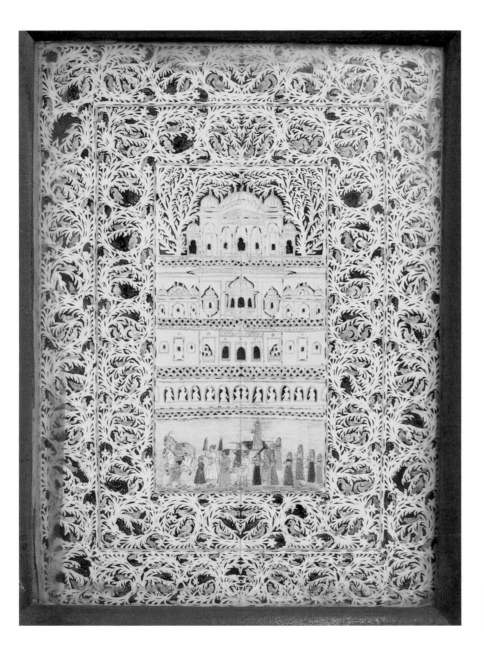

A paper-cut by
Maharaja Pratap
Singh

EDUCATION AND SPORTS

The patronage of learning and the personal acquisition of knowledge are both central to traditional Indian conceptions of kingship. A famous treatise on statecraft entitled *Shukraniti* advises that the king should associate with a guru in order to learn the *shastras* because 'a king who is trained in the branches of learning is respected by the good'. Furthermore 'the king should always take such steps as may advance the arts and sciences of the country,' notably by amply rewarding those who excel in them. Such people include 'those who are proficient in the revealed literature (the Vedas) … those who are well-versed in the Puranas, those who know the Shastras…,' astrologers, masters of Ayurveda, and all 'others who are meritorious, intelligent and masters of their passions – these classes of men the king should worship and maintain by stipends, gifts and honours.'

Though texts like *Shukraniti* were of course composed by learned pandits, it would be a mistake to dismiss their advice as self-interested special pleading. They refer to the contractual basis of Indian kingship. Rulers like the Maharajas of Jaipur might have claimed divine descent but they did not rule by divine right. Their privileged position carried specific responsibilities, amongst which the promotion of learning ranked high. A king's palace was not only a centre of government but a centre of scholarship as well. In this chapter we examine the education (including physical exercise) of successive rulers of Jaipur and their efforts to promote learning and sport amongst their people.

The Eighteenth Century

Of all the Rajput maharajas of the Mughal era, Sawai Jai Singh II stands out as the most accomplished intellectually. He is especially remembered by posterity as an astronomer and as the builder of observatories. According to his own account, he developed

A perspective view of the Jantar Mantar in Banaras, made by an East India Company engineer, Lt. Col. Archibald Campbell, c. 1770

Facing page: The Samrat Yantra

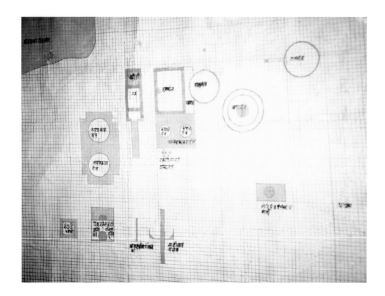

this interest at an early age: in the preface to his major treatise on the subject he describes himself as one who 'from the first dawning of reason in his mind' devoted himself to the solution of mathematical problems; and he claims that God, the 'supreme artificer', rewarded his arduous study of astronomy by granting him 'a thorough knowledge of its principles and rules'.

To learn the subject properly he associated with a guru, a south Indian pandit named Jagannath (whom he later rewarded with a grant of land). Their studies focussed on the Arabic and the Indian traditions. They were also familiar with classical European ideas (notably those of Euclid and Ptolemy) which had long been incorporated within Arabic scholarship; and they had access to some modern European works, including those of Flamsteed and La Hire. In all of the works that they studied they found that the computational tables, by which one could predict the position of heavenly bodies, were in varying degrees inaccurate. Ancient Brahminical texts such as the *Brahma Siddhanta* and the more recent tables of the Central Asian 'astronomer king' Ulugh Beg were equally unreliable. They attributed the errors to the use of inadequate instruments and sought to correct them by designing and constructing their own, on a massive scale. The fruits of their labour were the five Jantar Mantars or observatories that they built in Delhi, Jaipur, Mathura, Ujjain and Banaras, and the composition of their own book of tables, entitled *Zij Muhammad Shahi*, that they presented to the Mughal Emperor (to whom it is dedicated and after whom it is named) in 1728.

The locations of the observatories are significant. The one in Delhi (possibly the first to be built, in 1724) was sited in a suburb outside the imperial city, an area known as Jaisinghpura that had been acquired in the previous century by Sawai Jai Singh's ancestor and namesake Maharaja Jai Singh I. This site was selected because Sawai Jai Singh's efforts to make more accurate observations and thus to reform the calendar were undertaken with the emperor's sanction. Mathura and Ujjain are both pilgrimage cities with which Sawai Jai Singh had connections through his imperial service. The remaining two – those in Banaras and in Jaipur itself – were built in palace areas: the first on the roof of the palace that his ancestor Raja Man Singh had constructed on the banks of the Ganges, the latter within the precincts of the City Palace. These locations associate Sawai Jai Singh's activities very directly with his religion and with government. Astronomy for him was not some hobby, to indulge in a space set aside for the purpose,

An 18th-century plan of the Jantar Mantar

but something conducted at the heart of his administration.

It is a measure of how advanced Sawai Jai Singh and Jagannath became in the field that soon after their deaths their accomplishments were remembered but no longer understood. Those who came after could not match them. While investigating Brahmin knowledge of astronomy in Banaras in 1772 (less than 30 years after Sawai Jai Singh's death), Sir Robert Barker was shown the observatory atop Man Singh's palace; but although the instruments were well preserved his guides could evidently give him little accurate information about their history:

> I was then conducted to an ancient building of stone, the lower part of which, in its present situation, was converted into a stable for horses, and a receptacle for lumber; but, by the number of courtyards and apartments, it appeared that it must once have been an edifice for the use of some public body of people. We entered this building, and went up a staircase to the top part of it, near to the river Ganges, that led to a large terrace, where, to my surprise and satisfaction, I saw a number of instruments yet remaining, in the greatest preservation, stupendously large, immoveable from the spot, and built of stone, some of them being upwards of twenty feet in height; and, although they are said to have been erected two hundred years ago [actually less than fifty], the graduations and divisions on the several arcs appeared as well cut, and as accurately divided, as if they had been the performance of a modern artist. The execution in the construction of these instruments exhibited a mathematical exactness in the fixing, bearing and fitting of the several parts, in the necessary and sufficient supports to the very large stones that composed them, and in the joining and fastening [of] each into the other by means of lead and iron.

Consistent with the inaccurate dating of them to two hundred years before, he was wrongly informed that the instruments had been built by the Emperor Akbar. Researching the same subject twenty years later, William Hunter was able to identify the correct patron because he was shown a copy of the *Zij*, but his chief informant, who was Jagannath's grandson, complained that no one cared about this kind of knowledge any more.

An 18th-century plan of Man Singh's palace in Banaras

107

Hunter was responsible for propagating the view of Sawai Jai Singh as a sort of
Indian Galileo: a man struggling against religious superstition in an effort to introduce
'scientific truth derived from a foreign source'. A little earlier the Jesuit Father Joseph
Tieffenthaler had described him as 'fascinated by everything that emanates from Europe,
and seeking out the acquaintance of foreigners'. Reinforced by 19th-century authors (and
later by Jawaharlal Nehru), this view of Sawai Jai Singh persists even today, but it is based
on a misconception. It inappropriately transfers to 18th-century India a European post-
Enlightenment paradigm that pits science against religion. For Sawai Jai Singh there was
no dichotomy. Indeed the frequent references to 'the supreme artificer' in his own writings
make it clear that his religion, far from being an obstacle, was the chief motivation for
his study. He sought to observe the movements of planets and positions of stars because
he believed that these dictate the fortunes of men. And though he was aware of the
Copernican model of the universe he never abandoned the orthodox Hindu view of the
earth as its fixed centre. It is true that a number of foreigners (especially Jesuits) visited
and even stayed in Jaipur from an early date, but they contributed less to his research than
is sometimes assumed. It would be more accurate to regard Sawai Jai Singh's activities as
an attempt to carry to perfection one of the traditional duties of a Hindu king.

In this regard, his involvement in astronomy is directly comparable to his sponsorship
of certain Vedic rituals. The patronage of temples and of the rituals routinely performed
in them was of course a normal activity for any Hindu ruler (and indeed for most
householders), but Sawai Jai Singh took this role a good deal further through the public
performance of rare and ancient *yajnas* which traditionally were the exclusive preserve

of paramount kings and emperors. Early in his reign, in January 1709, to celebrate the recapture of Amber from Mughal forces following the battle of Sambhar, he sponsored a performance of the Vajpey Yajna, a ritual that involves feeding the Gods with *soma*, a juice extracted from a creeper. Later, in August 1734 and again in July 1742, he twice sponsored the Ashvamedh Yajna. This entails allowing a horse to roam freely through the state, to signal its limitless borders, then recapturing and sacrificing it. Both rituals involve the employment of learned priests to perform them (notably in this case Sawai Jai Singh's *rajguru* Ratnakar Dikshit) and of other pandits to commemorate the events in specially commissioned texts. Vishwanath Ranade, a priest and author from Banaras was engaged to write an account of the Vajpey Yajna, and his text, besides chronicling the details of the ritual, lays stress on the participation of many learned men whose 'poverty was relieved' by Sawai Jai Singh's frequent and generous payments.

About the education of Ishvari Singh, Sawai Jai Singh's elder son and immediate successor, little is known except that the person responsible for supervising it was the *diwan*, Vidyadhar, from which we might infer not only that great importance was attached to his schooling but also that it was specifically tailored to prepare him to govern.

A poem in praise of Maharaja Pratap Singh (r. 1778-1803), composed by Krishna Datta, gives us some insight into life in the City Palace at the end of the 18th century. Although the existence of the poem is in itself evidence of the continued patronage

of men of learning, in his account of the maharaja's daily routine, Krishna Datta places less emphasis on education than on the ruler's patronage of music and his participation in sports. He describes how, towards the end of his daily morning visit to the temple of Govind Dev, the maharaja might be approached by the *darogha* of the *filkhana* (director of the elephant stables), and be informed about some elephants that were in rut and out of control. The maharaja would then give orders for a fight to be arranged, and be carried

Portrait of Maharaja
Ram Singh II,
wearing a *mizrab*

110

in his palanquin along covered corridors to the Moti Burj overlooking the Chaugan, to watch it proceed. But this is not a royal indulgence alone: the common people assemble in thousands to watch as well. Afterwards, the maharaja is conveyed along further passages to the Atish or horse stables, situated in the south-western part of the palace area. Here he plays polo with some of the nobles. The poet's implication is that the game is played within the stable yard, and that the maharaja is in this case not a spectator but a participant.

The Nineteenth Century

The early decades of the 19th century appear not to have been a high point for the life of learning in the Jaipur court. The contemporary English historian of the Rajputs, James Tod, complained that Maharaja Jagat Singh (r. 1803-18) sold off parts of Sawai Jai Singh's celebrated library in order to raise cash to lavish on his favourite concubine, Ras Caphoor, and he roundly condemned this ransacking of 'the noble treasures of learning'. Matters did not improve in the time of his son and successor, Maharaja Jai Singh III (r. 1819-35) who succeeded to the *gaddi* at birth but whose reign throughout was a period of minority, where the young ruler was dominated by his mother, acting as regent, and by Jhuta Ram, her minister. The French scientist Victor Jacquemont visited Jaipur in March 1832, when the Maharaja was nearly 13, and described Jhuta Ram's scheme for his ruler's education:

> He takes great care to keep him in cotton wool and to prevent him from learning Persian. He is taught Sanskrit and is shown how to string a bow within the confines of his apartment, but this is the most martial of the exercises he is permitted to engage in. This educational regime is not lacking in alcohol and opium, to make the child an imbecile.

As Maharaja Ram Singh II (r. 1835-80) also came to throne as an infant, the reins of power were again held by the ruler's mother. Within a few years the British grew impatient with the unpredictable nature of *zanana* influence in this newly allied state, and by 1839 they had wrested control of the regency council by installing their Resident as its chairman. When John Ludlow was appointed Resident in 1844 he extended his authority to include the management of Ram Singh's education. The syllabus he designed contrasts sharply with the one that had been drawn up earlier by Jhuta Ram for Jai Singh III. No doubt Ludlow was motivated largely by the interests of the East India Company, but where Jhuta Ram's tutelage aimed to make the ruler for ever dependent on his ministers, Ludlow's equipped him to think and act independently. Ram Singh was taught Urdu and English as well as Sanskrit and the vernacular Dhundhari, so that he could manage state papers and converse with his allies as well as enjoy his own classical and folk heritage. Lessons in political history and administration were delivered personally by the Resident himself. In spite of (perhaps even because of) his small physique, Ram Singh was taught to ride, to shoot and to fence. And to render his appreciation of music more informed, he

learned to play the *sitar* and the *veena*. Portraits of him in middle age show him wearing a *mizrab*, a musician's plectrum-ring, suggesting that at least some of these early lessons were continued into adult life.

Ludlow's ideas regarding education did not stop with the ruler, but were extended towards other citizens of Jaipur. With the support of Pandit Shiv Deen he persuaded the young Ram Singh to found a college in the city, to provide the sons of the priestly and

Maharaja's College; photograph by Colin Murray for Bourne & Shepherd

112

mercantile classes with a formal education. The Maharaja's College opened in 1844 in a newly-completed temple building immediately opposite the Hawa Mahal on Sireh Deodhi Bazaar. It started as a secondary school, teaching Sanskrit, Urdu and English to some 40 pupils under the supervision of Shiv Deen.

From this point onwards the story of education in Jaipur moves outside the walls of the City Palace, but the matter remained a central concern of palace authorities. As the

Mahararaja's College and other schools founded subsequently flourished and grew, the palace retained responsibility for the recruitment and appointment of teaching staff, who in turn submitted their annual reports to the Durbar, and the treasury paid the bills. Public education became, in short, a function of government and an instrument by which the palace could forge the state's future prosperity.

By 1852 the Maharaja's College had grown to the point where it was necessary to divide it internally, with the foundation of a separate Sanskrit College, under Hari Das Shastri. By 1865, pressure on space in the building necessitated the removal of the Sanskrit College to its own site, another temple building further down the same road, the Ramachandra Temple. The number of pupils rose steadily: by 1875 there were 800 in the Maharaja's College and 200 in the Sanskrit College, and they continued to rise thereafter. This increase reflects the growing public acceptance of centralized education. Later in the century, the Colleges expanded to include higher as well as secondary education, with the introduction of BA degrees in 1890 and Masters degrees in 1896. This occasioned another swell in numbers as individual students attended them for longer periods.

Some insight into the administration, curriculum and teaching style of the Maharaja's College can be gained from the Principal's report to the Durbar of 1881. At this time the College taught over 800 boys aged between 9 and 22. None paid any fees. The total cost to the state treasury of running the College was Rs 21,000 per annum, which means the cost of educating one pupil was Rs 26 and 4 annas. The College was subdivided into three departments – English, Hindi and Persian – each of which comprised several classes. An individual pupil tended to stay in one department (its language being not only its main

A 'gallery' classroom of the Sanskrit College, housed in the Ramachandra temple

114

subject but the medium of instruction), though some progressed from the Hindi to the English department. The best students went on to university at Calcutta or Lahore.

Though justly proud of his high-achievers, the Principal, Dinanath Mukerjee, was no less attentive to the beginners:

> In the lowest Gallery class [so called because its classroom was an open veranda], the boys receive lessons on lines and plane figures [i.e. geometry], and learn to count numbers, and add or subtract, by means of the abacus. Instruction is also imparted on the natural history of animals, most familiar to them. The various physical movements recommended by Mr Stow are found extremely useful in securing discipline in the class, and making the boys attend to what the teacher has to say. As it is impossible for boys to remain in the same posture, attending to the same subject, for a whole hour, they naturally grow restless and noisy, and the physical movements, which the boys simultaneously perform at the instance of the teacher, serve at once to restore order in the class.

By the second year, this synchronized P.E. is apparently no longer necessary, and attention is paid to moral education:

> The boys of the second Gallery class receive lessons in Natural History, Mental Arithmetic and Geography, as well as on lines and plane figures … During one day in the week, the boys in the Gallery classes recite verses selected from poems on moral subjects. The teacher carefully explains these verses before the boys are required to get them by heart. He duly dilates upon every moral lesson contained in them and takes care to instil into their minds salutary moral precepts. [But in the break period, exercise and moral lessons are combined.] At one o'clock in the afternoon boys are allowed to recreate themselves for half an hour. Their conduct is watched over by the teachers while they are at play. The teacher's remaining with the boys in the playground is a great advantage, for it is there that he has the best opportunity of observing their character. In correcting the conduct of pupils the teacher addresses more to their understanding and moral feelings than to physical fear. … The majority of boys in a class cannot be wicked, and are susceptible to moral education. Their example cannot fail to correct the rest. As a rule, we have dispensed with the use of the ratan [cane], as tending to blunt the softer feelings. Nothing is so telling to a boy as when he stands convicted by his class-fellows, and nothing so encouraging and pleasing as when he is praised by the teacher before them for conduct worthy of praise.

Mukerjee admits that trusting in their innate goodness works better with younger boys (in spite of their apparently weak powers of attention) than with those who have entered

the College when older; but as those who have been subjected to this approach work their way up through the College the general ethos improves.

In his concluding remarks, the Principal emphasises the value of teaching English, deriding those who dismiss it as unnecessary in a place like Jaipur, where the population speaks Hindi and the administration is conducted in Urdu. Such a view, Mukerjee insists, is partial and short-sighted. For one thing, a knowledge of English is increasingly required for some of the offices of progressive states like Jaipur; but more importantly, a familiarity with 'the developed thoughts and doctrines of the enlightened West in the various departments of science and literature, as well as with the most wonderful discoveries and inventions, is of paramount importance for the moral and intellectual culture of the people of India.'

Mukerjee's belief in the benefits of English and his concern for the development of the people of all India, not just Jaipur, are both indications of his origin outside the state. As his name indicates, he was, of course, a Bengali – one of a number who were recruited especially by Maharaja Ram Singh, precisely because he could depend on them to impart

Maharaja Madho Singh II with advisers, including Sansar Chandra Sen and Samuel Swinton Jacon, to his left and right

this vision, which was still at this time uncommon in Jaipur. The unnamed adversaries to whom Mukerjee's comments were addressed no doubt included some of the more conservative members of the court.

There is a traditional saying in Jaipur, that the Rajput who learns to read forgets how to ride. In 1862, Ram Singh sought to combat this prejudice directly by establishing a Rajput School, exclusively for the sons of nobles. It opened with just 32 reluctant pupils. The headmaster was another recruit from Bengal, Sansar Chandra Sen. It is a measure of the proximity of state education to the government that Sen was later appointed private secretary to the maharaja's successor, Madho Singh II (r. 1880-1922). Yet another Bengali recruit (to the staff of the Maharaja's College), Kanti Chander Mukerjee, later became Madho Singh's prime minister. The state's connection with Bengal goes back to the 16th century when Raja Man Singh I served as the Mughal governor there and returned with the *murti* of Shila Devi and a retinue of pandits; but in the 19th century this long-established traffic was revitalized and given a new focus.

If Ram Singh's plans for education could include even his fellow Rajputs, girls were not forgotten. A Central Girls School was opened in 1867 with 200 pupils up to the age of 16. Like the boys of the Maharaja's College, they were mostly from the Brahmin and Bania communities. There was also a Female Industrial School where widows could learn needlework and other skills from which they could earn a living. By the early 1880s there were as many as 11 girls schools in the city, with a combined total of nearly 800 pupils, centrally managed by another recruit from outside, this one a British teacher named Jane Joyce.

In the rural districts outside the city there were 44 schools by the mid 1880s, with over a thousand pupils between them. In general, people were quick to take advantage of this state provision: 15 years later, the total number of pupils in state schools had reached 16,000, though the number of female students had remained static, showing that some traditions die hard. What the state could not manage with its own resources it achieved by what would now be called outsourcing: students were sent at state expense to Thomason College in Roorkee to learn engineering, and to the Forest Research Institute in Dehra Dun to learn conservation. Female medical students were sent to Agra to learn gynaecology. Ram Singh also supported the British initiative to educate Rajput nobles through the establishment of Mayo College in Ajmer. He contributed towards the cost, encouraged his *thakurs* to send their sons there and built for their accommodation a Jaipur Boarding House in the college grounds, even before the main buildings were completed.

For the benefit of those of his subjects who were already above school age, Ram Singh opened a Public Library in 1866. The kind of knowledge that this institution was intended to impart among his citizens is apparent from some of the books that he personally donated. They include, for example, a clutch of works on the new science of electricity, including Michael Faraday's three-volume *Experimental Researches in Electricity* (1839-55), Auguste de la Rive's three-volume *Treatise on Electricity* (1853-8), Alfred Garratt's

Medical Electricity (1866) and Robert Sabine's *The Electric Telegraph* (1867). These books were at some point returned to the City Palace library, where they remain.

Perhaps the most far-sighted of Ram Singh's educational policies – in terms of the state's developing economy – was his cultivation of the industrial arts. As early as 1847, when he was still under the tutelage of John Ludlow, he had sent five craftsmen to the Bombay Polytechnic Institute to learn pottery. But in 1866 he went much further by establishing a School of Arts in Jaipur. This offered practical training in such arts as pottery, sculpture, carpentry and wood-carving, engraving, drawing and metalwork, including the inlay of gold on steel (*koft gari*). The School was originally intended for boys of the traditional artisan classes, but the employment opportunities it offered quickly attracted a wider social range of pupils. Most prestigious was the drawing department, some of whose graduates secured posts as draughtsmen in the office of the state's executive engineer. Commercially most successful was the pottery department: according to the Bengali principal, Opendronath Sen, in 1877, 'the glazed earthen articles, the imitation fruits, the native figures like those made in Lucknow, the white clay goblets, and many other useful and ornamental things that are turned out by the boys of this class meet with ready sale.'

Some of the School's departments interacted or competed with existing local industries. Thus the wood-carving department 'was opened solely to improve the art of printing chintz' – a reference to the wood-block printed textiles that are a speciality of Sanganer. The marble figures produced by the sculpture department, 'though expensive, are far superior to those sold in the bazaar. The pupils are now engaged in making some large figures of Hindu idols'. Somewhat less market-conscious was the head of the clock-making department: 'a mysterious clock altogether on a new principle was made by him during the last year … it now adorns the drawing room in His Highness's palace'. The maharaja may have been the only taker for the quirky clocks, but the School's other products fared better. The various functional and ornamental items made in brass and silver, lacquer and enamelware were advertised in an illustrated catalogue that gave details of dimensions and prices. The income generated from the sale of these goods was almost a quarter of the total cost of running the School, with the remainder being covered by a treasury grant.

A related institution that was developed in the reign of Maharaja Madho Singh II, the Jaipur Museum, equally played a role in the state's broad education policy. It had its origin in a proposal from the Residency surgeon, Dr Thomas Holbein Hendley, to establish an Economic and Industrial Museum. In a letter to the Durbar in November 1880, he spelt out his views on the nature and social purpose of such an establishment: a museum, he said,

> should not be a mere collection of stones and minerals, of rare birds and
> animals, or of old and curious articles only interesting to an antiquary, but it
> should be a means of educating and amusing the common people. It should

be a place, for instance, where a man can see the best kind of well gear, or the most useful form of plough – where he can find specimens of all sorts of seeds and manures, with their prices and estimated value – where he can improve his mind by study of machinery, or by examining the products and manufactures of other countries than his own.

The Durbar was happy to give its consent to this plan and Hendley immediately began to assemble exhibits that were initially displayed in temporary premises near the City Palace. To assist him he recruited a committee that included the state engineer, Swinton Jacob, the former schoolmaster Sansar Chandra Sen, one Pandit Braj Ballabh, to act as head clerk, and – in spite of his comments on birds and animals – a taxidermist.

During the first three months of its opening, at the end of 1881, the fledgling museum was visited by around 200 people per day; but in the New Year the numbers suddenly took off, reaching an average of 5,000 per day. 'No doubt the majority of visitors have come from mere motives of curiosity, and because no charge is made for admission,' conceded an obviously delighted Hendley; 'but none seem disappointed, and many come again to examine the collections at more leisure.' Furthermore the crowds showed their intelligent interest in their orderly behaviour: even on one day when the attendance exceeded 10,000 nothing was broken. In arranging the display, Hendley remained true to his manifesto: the exhibits included some models of English vegetables, presented by Sutton & Sons of Reading. 'The giant cauliflowers and the magnificent peas, tomatoes and carrots astonish the Jaipur agriculturalist.' One can imagine.

Hendley's next related initiative, the Jaipur Exhibition of 1883, was focussed more exclusively on the industrial arts, but this too had a social and didactic purpose. The declared intention of the exhibition was not just to display the arts of Jaipur and other regions, but to improve the taste of the citizens by showing them what was worthy of being admired, and to hone the skills of craftsmen by presenting them with objects worthy of imitation. The exhibition did much to raise Jaipur's profile within India and abroad, to attract custom to its commercial arts. But, meanwhile, back home it was intended as a direct intervention in the process of production: 'to present to the craftsmen selected examples of the best art work of India, in the hope that they might profit thereby'.

When the Albert Hall in Ram Niwas Gardens was completed and formally opened in 1887, the contents of the former Economic and Industrial Museum were combined with many of the items from the Jaipur Exhibition to form the core collection of a new and permanent Jaipur Museum. All of the educational functions of those earlier displays were continued by the new one. The first of the Museum's declared purposes (as recorded in Hendley's report) was 'to amuse and instruct the common people who have no shop windows to gaze into as in Europe and who have so little to interest them in their daily lives'. It was also intended, 'to enable workmen to see good specimens of art', to educate Jaipur's youth, and 'to promote trade'. The models of fruit and vegetables were still there, now complemented by anatomical and other scientific diagrams and specimens. Indeed,

there was enough, in Hendley's estimation, 'to illustrate every ordinary branch of learning in such a way as to facilitate the attainment of a University degree in any subject.' He had hopes that the museum would work in concert with the Maharaja's College to provide a general education, and he arranged that portions of the galleries could be closed off so that classes could be conducted in them without disturbing other visitors.

Though Hendley's ambitions of a formal collaboration with other institutions were not fulfilled, the museum did play a central role in public education. During its first 12 years it welcomed three million visitors through its turnstiles. Some amongst these were foreigners, whose appreciation helped the museum to gain international recognition; but the vast majority were Jaipur's own citizens – men, women and children in equal numbers – visiting again and again this object of wonder, instruction and delight.

The Twentieth Century

Since Madho Singh was already an adult at the time of his adoption by Maharaja Ram Singh, there was no opportunity to subject him to the rigorous educational programme that his predecessor had undergone.   By comparison, his earlier education had been somewhat scanty.   He had briefly attended the Rajput School in Jaipur – following the advice of Ram Singh to the boy's natural father, long before the adoption – but he had not liked it and soon ran away to join an *akhada* or wrestling school, in his home town of Isarda. A little later the influence of a sympathetic *guru* in Vrindavan had gone some way towards opening his eyes to the rewards of intellectual pursuits, but a formal syllabus was

The Albert Hall or Jaipur Museum

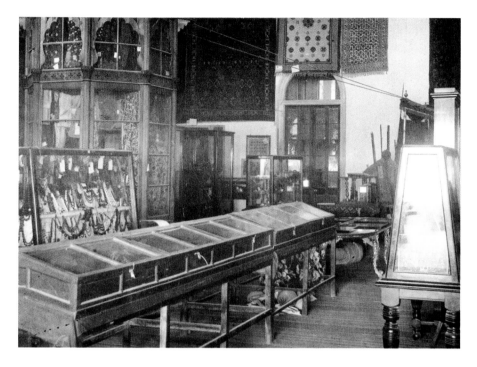

still lacking. Recording this career, his biographer Hanuman Sharma acknowledged that many in Jaipur considered Madho Singh uneducated; but from the events of his reign it is evident that he had innate intelligence and sound judgment. With the help of well-chosen advisers he skilfully handled relations with the British during the changing times of the early 20th century, before and after the First World War.

Madho Singh oversaw the development of state education through the expansion of the institutions founded by his predecessor, as described. He also held firm views about the proper content and balance of education that were consistent with his other ideas regarding the influence of European ideas. He once gave some advice to a Jaipur businessman named Ganesh Narayan Somani who was then responsible for the education of a young Jodhpuri nobleman, the Thakur of Nimaj. Seeing Somani with his pupil, Madho Singh called him over and said, 'Somaniji, you are a Vaishya and just as a Vaishya, putting weights in one scale and articles in the other, keeps the balance, never letting one scale of the balance outweigh the other, so you should give such tuition and training to the young chief that the scale of Western education may not outweigh our traditional manners and methods of the East.'

Madho Singh made these comments when he arrived in Bombay in 1902, on his return from attending the coronation of King Edward VII in London; and after spending several months in Britain he was perhaps suffering from a surfeit of Western ways and was missing the traditional manners of home. Somani recalled them 20 years later, and in return offered advice to the maharaja regarding the education of his recently adopted successor, Raj Kumar Man Singh. Somani argued against sending the boy to Mayo

Top left:
A gallery of the Jaipur Exhibition, held in1883

Top right:
A vase displayed in the exhibition

College in Ajmer, because such schools teach 'nothing higher and nobler than mere imitation of western fashions.' Ten years of study in such a place will not teach a prince his duties towards his people; it will only make him self-indulgent. Sending him to England would also make him too Westernized. Somani suggested instead that he should be sent to one of the public schools in Jaipur that had been founded by Ram Singh, where, like his future subjects, he could get a good grounding in both economics and the sacred books of Hinduism.

It was no doubt good advice but it was not heeded. The death of Madho Singh soon after the adoption ensured that it was the minority council, led by the British, who made the decisions about Man Singh's education. He was sent to Mayo College; and when he had finished with that, he was sent to England, to the Royal Military Academy

Maharaja Madho Singh II with the recently adopted Maharaj Kumar Man Singh, in 1921

in Woolwich (where he was the first ever Indian cadet). These were not institutions to cultivate bookishness and it was as a sportsman – most famously as a polo player – that Man Singh II gained renown. His interests in sports extended well beyond his personal participation. Infused with the English public school ethic of *mens sana in corpore sano*, he encouraged the development of a wide range of games in Jaipur. As we have mentioned elsewhere, his birthday celebrations regularly included hockey and football matches, and the palace Chaugan became a public stadium, the regular venue for matches of various kinds.

Maharaja's College, Jaipur.
Mr. R. T. Russell, F.R.I.B.A., Chief Architect, P.W.D., New Delhi.

Meanwhile the schools were not neglected. In 1932 the Maharaja's College was moved to new and larger premises outside the walled city. A design for the college buildings was supplied by Robert Tor Russell, the head of the New Delhi PWD who had designed several buildings in the new capital including Connaught Place (though the college as it stands today suggests some modifications to the design were made in the course of execution). In 1943, Man Singh's third wife, Maharani Gayatri Devi founded a girls' school. As we have seen, this was not quite the first girls' school in the city (as is sometimes supposed), but it was the first that was aimed particularly at the daughters of the nobility who continued to lead sheltered lives. As the Maharani herself recalled in her memoirs:

> I decided that the school should be primarily for the daughters of the noble families and the higher echelons of society, because it was their womenfolk who observed the rules of purdah most strictly. Among the middle classes girls were already being educated, but the nobility had quite different ideas and were far more hidebound in their lives.

The first headmistress, who served for thirty years, was a Scotswoman, Miss Lilian Lutter, who had taught in Burma during the Japanese invasion. The foundations she laid have proved enduring: still going strong over sixty years later, MGD School has made and continues to make a significant contribution to female secondary education in Rajasthan.

The most recent example of an initiative from the Palace to promote education in Jaipur is the establishment of a nursery school run on the Montessori system, by Maharaja Bhawani Singh's daughter, Princess Diya Kumari.

Robert Tor Russell's original design for the new Maharaja's College, 1929

123

GOVERNANCE

With its integration into the Indian Union in the years following Independence in 1947, the Jaipur state as an autonomous entity ceased to exist. In the course of the last two or three years of its existence, new legislative bodies were established which introduced for the first time some semblance or at least a fore-runner of democracy; but up until that point the maharaja had been an absolute ruler, and the City Palace was not only his principal ceremonial residence but also a seat of government. The palace was a court that had to accommodate the maharaja and the women of the *zanana*, and a variety of departments that served their immediate personal needs. But it was also amongst other things a treasury and tax office, a war cabinet, council chamber and judicial court.

The physical spaces within the palace compound that were reserved for these functions changed and developed over time. The judicial and advisory activities that required assemblies were usually conducted in the audience halls, while some of the personal and household offices and stores were probably housed in the Anand Mandir facing the Chandra Mahal. The more mundane tasks such as accounting and the workshops had shifting locations, but from 1884-5, when Jaleb Chowk was rebuilt, many of them were concentrated there. The large building, originally known as the Naya Mahal (later called the Sawai Man Singh Town Hall), had been built slightly earlier in that courtyard's south-east corner to house administrative departments. The Mubarak Mahal, in the palace's southern courtyard, was originally built as a reception room for visitors in 1900, but was soon reallocated to the Mahakma Khas, the maharaja's private office.

Many of the tasks addressed by these administrative departments – most importantly, the setting and collection of land revenue – related to activities in the state as a whole, outside the physical domain of the palace; but a description of them is included here to give a sense of the palace as a centre not only of court pageantry but of political administration. The last two decades of autonomous rule are unsurprisingly better documented than any earlier period, and the account that follows draws particularly on documents from the 1930s and '40s, though occasionally it looks back to show what had changed with the passage of time.

Group photograph of Lord Irwin and visiting party, late 1920s; in front of the Mubarak Mahal

Facing page: Portrait of a *thakur*, or noble c. 1800

Court and Council

Maharaja Sawai Ram Singh II introduced a Royal Council in 1867 to divide the responsibilities hitherto held in the hands of the prime minister. Earlier rulers had tended to depend on the support of a single individual, known either as the *diwan* or *mukhtar*. The change was designed to prevent a concentration of power (as had occurred during periods of minority rule) and to include a wider pool of talent; but the eight ministers of the council were still selected by the maharaja and remained members at his discretion, so the reform entailed no dilution of his own power of patronage.

By the 1930s little had changed. The maharaja was still the president of the now re-named Council of State. The vice-president was the de facto prime minister and was actually called such from 1937. Often this was a professional bureaucrat recruited from outside the state to ensure his impartiality: in the mid-1930s the post was filled by an Englishman, a retired officer of the Political Department of British India, Lt. Col. Sir Beauchamp St John, while those who followed him in the remaining years of autonomous rule included Raja Gyan Nath, Sir Mirza Ismail and Sir V.T. Krishnamachari. The remaining members of the council held specialist portfolios, covering finance, revenue, justice, home affairs, public works and education. Typically these posts were held by selected *thakurs* or by other specially recruited professionals. But they were not only a committee of technocrats; they also held a judicial function as the Council of State was Jaipur's highest court, and the Judicial Member of Council was also the state's Chief Justice. Despite the claim made in a report of 1935 that 'the administration of civil and criminal justice is now guided generally by the spirit of the law in force in British India', the separation of the judiciary and executive was acknowledged as a principle and only slowly enacted.

The Jaipur Penal Code necessarily reflected certain local realities, notably the need to protect the religious rights of the Muslim minority whilst recognizing that the overwhelming majority of citizens were Hindus. Thus, 'whoever, with deliberate intention of wounding the religious feelings of any person, utters any word or makes any sound in the hearing of that person or makes any gesture in the sight of that person or places any object in the sight of that person, shall be punished with imprisonment of either description [with or without hard labour] for a term which may extend to one year, or with a fine or with both'. But one could be imprisoned for up to 10 years for killing a cow and even punished for importing beef that had been slaughtered outside the state, while the killing of other creatures of sacred significance to Hindus – such as monkeys and peacocks – also incurred a hefty fine of Rs 50.

The Penal Code contained a number of provisions to protect public health and morals, including the following prohibition on obscenity: 'Whoever sells or distributes, imports or prints for sale or hire, or wilfully exhibits to public view, any obscene book, pamphlet, paper, drawing, painting, representation or figure, or attempts or offers to do so, shall be punished with imprisonment...for a term which may extend to three months, or with a fine

or with both.' But the ban contains an interesting exception: 'This section does not extend to any representation sculptured, engraved, painted or otherwise represented, on or in any temple, or on any car used for the conveyance of idols, or kept or used for any religious purpose.' It can hardly be supposed that the Jaipur government's intention in making this exception was to signal that they would tolerate obscenity in temples. Rather, it reveals their awareness that some sacred images might appear obscene to some sensibilities. And the exception pre-empts a possible line of defence: it would not be possible for a defendant to argue that his smutty pictures should not be deemed obscene on the ground that much worse was displayed in sacred art.

Land Revenue

The population of the state according to the 1931 census was 26 lakhs (2.6 million), making it the most populous state in Rajputana, and the fifth most populous in India.

The Sabha Niwas in the Palace, prepared for a durbar, 1876

127

Apart from Jaipur city itself the largest towns were all in Shekhawati district: they were Sikar, Fatehpur, Nawalgarh, Jhunjhunu and Lachmangarh. But the division of the state into districts for the purposes of land revenue was drawn along geographical lines, not by population. There were 11 such districts or *nizamats*, in two groups. The western group included the centre: Jaipur itself, and Amber and Torawati to its north, as well as the populous Shekhawati as a single district, Sambhar to the west (bordering Jodhpur) and Malpura to the south-west. The eastern group included Dausa, Sawai Madhopur, Gangapur, Hindaun and the isolated pocket of Kot Kasim. Much of the land within these *nizamats* actually belonged to the *thikanas* and was controlled by the *thakurs*, the maharaja's clansmen and nobles of the court; so while the total area of the state was in excess of 16,000 square miles, the area of *khalsa* land, from which revenue was paid directly to the state treasury, accounted for less than 5,000 square miles.

Each of the two groups of *nizamats* was managed by a *diwan* who was answerable to the revenue member of the Council. Below the level of the *diwan*, each *nizamat* had its own *nazim* in charge, and at the very local level each *nizamat* was further subdivided into *tehsils* with a *tehsildar* responsible for the collection of revenue. It was a long chain that conveyed the peasant farmer's taxes to his maharaja. Nevertheless genuine efforts were made from time to time to improve the farmers' condition and to assist them in meeting the demands made of them. New settlement and survey operations were undertaken in 1923 'to secure for the cultivator a certain fixity of tenure and have the lands properly measured and a record of rights properly prepared'. At the same time the dates of tax collection were changed 'to give the tenant a reasonable time for the disposal of his out-turn at advantageous prices,' since previously 'early collection compelled some

Fatehpur, one
the towns of
Shekhawati

tenants to borrow at ruinous rates of interest or to part with their produce at low prices.' Unauthorized weights were banned in rural areas, and no rent was charged for land that was set aside for growing timber for fuel and building purposes. Later, in the 1930s, the state agricultural farm at Basi conducted research and experiments to improve the varieties of seed for all crops and vegetables, and to improve the cattle breeding stock. The farm also staged agricultural shows to demonstrate new implements: a report of 1939 shows 'a cultivator smilingly carrying away a modern plough bought after a demonstration by the Agricultural department'.

If this suggests a happy tale of constant improvement, reports also indicate an awareness that the periodic failure of the rains could quickly undo what had been achieved. In drought years, fodder and grain depots were opened throughout the state, where grain was sold at cost price and fodder at concession rates. Famine relief work was directed towards the improvement of irrigation, so that by the end of the 1930s the prime minister could boast that the state contained over 400 tanks and reservoirs – though he conceded that they were still insufficient.

Apart from humanitarian concerns, the importance of constantly improving the yield from the land is revealed by the budget statistics. According to the 1929 budget, a state investment of just Rs 7 lakhs produced a return to the treasury of over Rs 43 lakhs, accounting for half of the entire state income. The land revenue was more than twice as much as was received in customs and excise dues from the state's traders.

In view of the contribution of the peasant farmer to the state economy, it is perhaps unsurprising that one of the early actions of Sir Mirza Ismail, following his appointment as prime minister in June 1942, should have been to call an assembly of all the *nazims* and *tehsildars* and to lecture them on their duties. His preliminary investigations had led him to believe that there was much to be done:

> I find that the villages in the State are in a deplorable condition, and I have no doubt you agree with me. Are we going to let them remain like this? Of course not. It is the elementary duty of any administration worthy of the name to improve the living conditions in our villages and to see that the *ryot* [tenant farmer] does not starve. It is our duty, too, to lift him up educationally and socially. The Revenue Department can play a very useful part in the improvement of rural life, and I am very hopeful that it will do so. If an epidemic breaks out, you should be the first to know and inform the Government. If the cattle are suffering from lack of water or fodder, you should bestir yourselves and not wait for the Agricultural or Veterinary Department to move in the matter.

It is typical of any administrator to imply that nothing has been achieved before his own term of office, and although – no doubt – there were no more grounds for complacency on this perennial subject in 1942 than at any other time, it would be unjust to take at face value his implied judgment on his predecessors. Even so, Mirza Ismail's speech to the revenue officers is interesting for what it reveals (again by implication) about relations within the system of administration.

First, in exhorting the *tehsildars* to action, he appeals not to their better nature (perhaps supposing that faculty to be lacking) but to their loyalty to the maharaja and to their pride. Thus, 'it should be our constant aim and earnest endeavour to promote the happiness and prosperity of the people,' because this will 'attain for the administration a high place in the administrations in India,' and because 'this is His Highness' ambition and it is up to us to enable him to achieve it'. Secondly, in deploying his very considerable powers of oratory to define 'the principles which should guide all your actions,' he hints at a prevailing lack of communication as the main obstacle impeding the peasant:

> I would like you to be accessible to all and sundry. By being accessible you will be able to know their wants more easily, and will thus be in a better position to help them. Moreover, accessibility on the part of the higher officers is, perhaps, the simplest, the easiest, and the most effective way of minimizing if not altogether stopping corruption in the lower officials and of protecting the average citizens from the tyranny of the petty official …The qualities which you should display in dealing with the peasant…are sympathy, patience in listening to him and solicitude for his welfare and an earnest desire to grant his requests if they are reasonable.

Throughout the speech, Sir Mirza by turns flattered and coaxed the *tehsildars*, calling them 'the back-bone of the administration,' and assuring him of his confidence that their whole-hearted assistance would be 'forthcoming in ample measure'. And he practised what he preached, making it his habit to deny audience to no citizen who requested it. But it may fairly be questioned whether his words and his example had the effect he hoped on the general levels of communication.

Services and Infrastructure

After land revenue, the next largest item on the Council's agenda in financial terms was public works. Under this heading came the construction of roads and railways, the provision of water and electricity and (a comparatively minor part of the cost) the design and construction of public buildings. By comparison with land revenue, public works were a net cost item. For example, in the 1929 budget, public works accounted for over 30% of the total state expenditure for the year (Rs 30.6 lakhs out of a total spend of 1 crore), while only a very small proportion of this figure was expected to be recouped, through the charging of rent on state-owned shop premises and the sale of land in the city for people to build houses. The fact that the budget includes proceeds from the sale of seeds and vegetables cultivated in Ram Niwas Gardens suggests that every effort was made to generate an income stream; but the costs involved were overwhelming. A report

of 1939 celebrates the extension of the Shekhawati rail network with the completion of lines connecting Jhunjhunu with Loharu and Sikar with Bissau, at a combined cost of Rs 57 lakhs, a figure equivalent to half of one year's entire budget.

Even relatively modest expenses such as building maintenance tended to be cumulative in nature: the more buildings that were constructed the more there were to maintain. The Jaipur state still paid for the upkeep of temples in Mathura and Vrindavan that had been built by the maharaja's ancestor, Raja Man Singh I, in the 16th century, besides maintaining temples in the city and paying for the periodic repair of the city wall. By comparison, the personal or domestic building works for the maharaja – such as extensions to the Rambagh Palace or the *chhatri* for the late Maharaja Madho Singh – were slight: the annual budget of the Raj Imarat (the specialist department responsible for such works) was just Rs 2 lakhs in the late 1920s, a figure that covered both staff salaries and building costs.

Jaipur railway station in the late 1920s, decked to receive Viceroy Lord Irwin

Two other significant cost items on the Council's agenda were medicine and education, and again as these services were developed the costs became cumulative. The first general hospital in the city, named after the Viceroy Lord Mayo, opened in 1875. The Zenana Hospital outside Chand Pol followed in 1931 and the Lady Willingdon Hospital on Rambagh Road in 1939. In the interval over fifty small hospitals or dispensaries had been founded in the districts. In the century following the opening of the Maharaja's College in 1844, the profusion of state-sponsored schools and colleges was a source of both pride and alarm. The initial running cost of the Maharaja's College was a meagre Rs 21,000 per year; within a hundred years, compulsory education was being introduced, the number of students in the state had crossed 60,000 and the annual cost had soared to Rs 12 lakhs. Every detail of expenditure was minutely accounted for. The budget for 1929 mentions two *chowkidars*, a peon, a *bhishti*, two housemaids and two sweepers who together comprised the menial staff employed at the Jaipur boarding house at Mayo College, and whose combined annual salary was Rs 984. Evidently, the accountants at the City Palace were assiduous.

Palace Departments

The *chhatri* or cenotaph of Maharaja Madho Singh II at Gaitor

An administration report from the mid-1930s shows the continuance into the modern era of a number of specialist service departments within the palace that had existed since its foundation. Indeed some of them had been re-established by Maharaja Sawai Jai Singh II on the basis of earlier departments that had served

his predecessors at Amber. While the Council of State's preoccupations changed and developed with the times, the household management of the palace was remarkably static.

Chief amongst these domestic departments, in terms of its proximity to the royal person, was the Kapadwara or state wardrobe. Located within the precincts of the Chandra Mahal, it had four sub-sections: the Jawahar Khana, a store for state jewellery and valuable ornaments; the Tosha Khana, for the maharaja's personal attire; the Zagar Khana, for gold and silver objects; and the Khazana Bela for cash. While within the confines of the palace, the maharaja was protected by the Risala Kalan; or at least he was nominally so, for as the report concedes this outfit was 'military in name only'. It was a dismounted body of 126 Rajputs who performed watch and guard duties within the palace, armed with swords and 'muzzle-loading guns of local manufacture'. Not that they were really expected to use these weapons: the report states frankly that their chief function was to grace ceremonial occasions as *lawazma* – literally 'paraphernalia'. The Mistri Khana was still maintained 'for the prompt manufacture and supply of articles of furniture required for the palaces.'

In the financial year 1933-4, 13 horses were added to the Atish (royal stables); and the removal of the same number and the death of two more left the total at the end of the year at 70, incurring an annual expenditure of Rs 46,000. One new purchase for the Shutar Khana increased the number in the camel stables from five to six (annual maintenance cost: Rs 2,700). The number of elephants in the Feel Khana remained unchanged at 16 (costing Rs 33,000). The costs had gone up and the numbers of animals

Mayo Hospital, opened in 1875; the statue of the former Viceroy after whom the hospital was originally named has been removed.

133

had almost certainly gone down but in other respects the activities of these departments were unchanged since the 18th century.

The Shikar Khana continued to record the number of wild animals shot in the year by the maharaja (two tigers, one panther and a bear), and supervised the construction of motorable roads to the preferred hunting grounds.

The most obvious newcomer to the list of 36 *karkhanas* or workshops that had been instituted by Sawai Jai Singh was the Motor Department (replacing the original *palki khana* and the 19th-century *baggi khana*). At the start of the year the department contained 66 vehicles; but the superintendent (one Mr E. Mason) had received instructions to replace three, and with the one presented by the Thakur of Bissau the total now stood at 67. The department's running costs were Rs 155,000 per year: almost twice as much as was spent on the horses, elephants and camels put together. Newspaper advertisements from about this time show that an Austin 20 (49 hp) could be purchased in Jaipur for Rs 9,300, while the more modest Austin 7 (10 hp) would set one back only Rs 2,300. Not that many residents of the city were buying cars as yet: the previous maharaja had somewhat delayed the introduction of the fashion by his habit of commandeering motor cars that belonged to his subjects and charging them for the petrol.

Constitutional Change

The establishment and periodic reform of a State Council did not alter the fundamental nature of Jaipur's oligarchy: from the beginning to just before the end the state was run by the maharaja in consort with a handful of trusted *thakurs* and of appointed professionals. The political changes that were introduced in the closing years of princely rule were the responses to external pressure, exerted by the march of the people of British India towards independence and democracy.

The extent to which the maharajas in general hoped and expected the distinct identity of their states and their own rule to survive the transition of power within British India, from the Crown to the Congress, can be gauged by the Jaipur government's response to the Draft Instrument of Accession in 1935. The Government of India Act of that year contained a draft of a document that the maharajas would have to sign when acceding to the proposed Indian federation; it set out the precise areas and limits within which their own authority would be retained, and it invited their comments. The *Memorandum Containing the Views of the Jaipur State on the Draft Instrument of Accession* was written for Maharaja Man Singh II by his then prime minister, Sir Beauchamp St John, but it plainly reflects the collective view of the Council.

The memorandum's comments on all of the Act's provisions on such key issues as law-making, property inheritance, land-owning and extradition reveal that it was taken for granted that the Jaipur state would continue within its existing borders under the rule of the maharaja and his heirs; and even that it would continue to have some sort of relationship with the British Crown. Thus, for example, the memorandum insists that

'no land or other property shall be acquired in this State for any Federal purpose, either on behalf of His Majesty [i.e. the King Emperor] or on behalf of the Federal Railway Authority or any other authority of the Federation, except with the consent of the Ruler of this State'.

Some of the memorandum's other reservations, regarding what might have been thought comparatively minor matters, reveal a somewhat entrenched position. For example, the Jaipur government refused to countenance the discontinuance of its own coinage. The so-called *jharshahi* currency included a gold *mohur*, worth over Rs 30, which 'though not legal tender, circulates freely throughout Rajputana,' as an informal unit of exchange. The official *jharshahi* rupee was worth slightly more than the British Indian rupee, a situation that Jaipur merchants had long complained against, pointing out that it was inconvenient for cross-border trade. But in the memorandum, *jharshahi* was 'regarded as an attribute of rule and an expression of sovereignty, and the Jaipur Government are not prepared to part with this sovereign right'.

Similarly, Jaipur had its own postal system which operated within the state alongside offices of the Imperial Post, but quite separately, with 'no inter-change of mails etc.' – an

The Chandra Mahal with the courtyard of the Sarvato Bhadra in the foreground; photograph by Lala Deen Dayal

arrangement which the state government evidently thought desirable to retain. They also (perhaps more sensibly) wished to reserve complete ownership and control over ancient monuments and archaeological sites. Indeed the Jaipur government had something to say or to reserve about every single provision of the draft Act except those relating to shipping in coastal waters, the management of ports and other maritime matters. These they let pass without amendment; but as Jaipur has no coast they could hardly be thought lax in performing their duty on that score. As things turned out they need not have worried: this draft Act was an early round in a protracted process of negotiation that was interrupted by the Second World War, and the whole basis of the integration of the Princely States looked very different thereafter.

The stirrings of political change in Jaipur can be detected in a report written by Sir Beauchamp's successor, Raja Gyan Nath in 1939. This document was directed not towards Council but to an external audience. Its very first sentence combatively complains: 'Too often is the criticism heard in British India that the Rulers of Indian States care only for their personal comforts and entertainments, and while extracting as much as they can from their subjects, give little in return.' He does not say whether the allegation is levelled by the people or by the rulers of British India but he goes on to rebut it with a barrage of information about the development of agriculture, irrigation, medicine, education, transport and industry within Jaipur.

Most probably his intended audience was in fact the Congress Party, who were critical of the maharajas' absolute rule, as he takes pains to point out the mechanisms in place to temper it. The Council of State had in fact for some time received guidance from a Consultative Committee of Sardars and listened to advice from a Legislative Committee; but as the first of these bodies comprised four leading *thakurs* and the second was made up of a mixture of *thakurs* and Council members, the extent to which they widened access to power might be questioned. Gyan Nath points out that these committees have been augmented by the recent establishment of District Advisory Boards that are 'broadly based and provide for the representation of all interests and classes'. Furthermore, direct contact with the needs of the people was achieved through the procedure of Zabani Arzies (or verbal requests): 'Every office, both at headquarters and in the Districts, has a petition box hung outside and at the end of the day the presiding officer personally opens these boxes, calls the petitioners and deals with each petition'. Painstaking as the

A reception by Boy Scouts during a visit to Jaipur by Dr Rajendra Prasad, first President of independent India in 1951 process sounds, Nath's conclusion that 'the question of securing for the people in a progressive manner close contact and association with Administration is under consideration,' was a claim hardly likely to impress those seeking moves towards democracy.

A decade later Jaipur had made some further progress down that road. In 1948 the Indian National Congress held its annual session in Jaipur (the first such session to be held since Independence and the first in an Indian state). To coincide with the event the Jaipur Government published a volume of photographs by Henri Cartier-Bresson, entitled *Beautiful Jaipur*, with views of the famous and now historic city, and of a recent royal wedding. The accompanying text by Max Oliver

stressed the convergence of tradition and modernity: Oliver insisted that it was 'only in Jaipur that I felt the unfathomed spirituality of India,' while he was equally impressed by 'the hospitals, snow-white and radiant with cleanliness'. No pressing need for change then, the booklet implied.

Another pamphlet issued by the Jaipur Government on this same occasion nevertheless sets out what changes had been made or attempted. It contains a note written by Altaf Ahmad Kherie, the Revenue member of the Jaipur State Council and its special 'Reforms Adviser'. He records how a 'Constitutional Reforms Committee', appointed by the maharaja to find ways of leading the people of Jaipur towards self-government, had started its work in November 1942. The following spring, the committee recommended the establishment of a Legislative Council to frame laws and a Representative Assembly 'for ventilating public grievances'. After a delay for due consideration these two new bodies were formed by proclamation by the Maharaja on New Year's Day 1944; but it was not until September of the following year that they were actually inaugurated, and whilst opening them the maharaja commented, with seeming complacency, 'We do not find in this constitutional development the consummation of democracy'. The members of the new bodies clearly shared that view: in March 1946 the Legislative Council passed a resolution calling for full responsible government in the state. They were not to get it, however, in the form they imagined, for the accession to India that eventually ushered in democratic rule saw also the disappearance of the autonomous Jaipur state.

Maharaj Kumar Bhawani Singh at a reception for politicians in the early 1950s

137

KACHCHWAHA DYNASTY

Bhar Mal r. 1548-1574

Bhagwan Das r. 1574-1589   Harika m. Akbar

Man Singh I r. 1589-1614

Jagat Singh   **Bhau Singh r. 1614-1621**

Maha Singh

Jai Singh I (Mirza Raja) r. 1621-1667

Ram Singh I r. 1667-1689

Kishan Singh

Bishan (Vishnu) Singh r. 1689-1699

Sawai Jai Singh II r. 1699-1743

Ishvari Singh r. 1743-50   **Madho Singh I r. 1750-1768**

Prithvi Singh r. 1768-1778   **Pratap Singh r. 1778-1803**

(1768-1779: Chundawat regency)

Jagat Singh r. 1803-1819

Jai Singh III r. 1819-1835

(1819-1835: Bhattiyani regency)

Ram Singh II r. 1835-1880

(1835-1851: Chundawat regency)

Madho Singh II r. 1880-1922

Man Singh II r. 1922-1949   (d. 1970)

(1922-1931: Regency council)

Bhawani Singh (b. 1931)

ACKNOWLEDGEMENTS

The sources for this book include a series of court histories commissioned by successive maharajas from Sawai Jai Singh II in the 18th century to the last maharaja with ruling powers, Sawai Man Singh II, in the 1940s, together with the records and reports of the various state departments that are now contained in the archives of the City Palace museum. A full list of these sources is given in the Bibliography. We are grateful to Maharaja Bhawani Singh who first suggested that we should write this book, and to the authorities of the City Palace and the curators of the Maharaja Sawai Man Singh II Museum who allowed us to study archival material and works of art on numerous occasions between 2002 and 2005. Special thanks are due to Narendra Singh, Himmat Singh, Pankaj Sharma, Sukhvir Singh and Sangeeta Dutta. We have benefited from suggestions and support from Rahaab Allana, Moya Carey, Sophie Gordon, Rima Hooja, Maurice Howard, Preetha Nair, Michelle O'Malley and Chandrakant Singh. We are also grateful to the British Academy and to the History of Art Department of the University of Sussex for grants which facilitated the archival research.

PHOTO CREDITS

Photographs by the authors: Pages 2, 3, 4-5, 7, 13, 17, 36, 38, 42, 43, 44, 45, 46, 47, 48, 49, 50, 52, 53, 54, 55, 56, 57 (bottom), 59, 60, 65 (top 3), 66, 67, 85, 90, 104, 108 (left), 109, 114, 120, 128 and 132.

Authors' collection: Pages 22, 80, 82, 83, 84, 89, 91, 100, 101, 105, 116, 121, 123, 124 and 135.

Drawings by Vibhuti Sachdev: Pages 41 and 51 (top).

Photographed or copied by RG Photographers, Jaipur, on commission for the authors, with the permission of Maharaja Sawai Man Singh II Museum, Jaipur City Palace: Pages 6, 8-9, 10, 11, 14, 15, 16, 20, 21, 23, 25, 26, 29, 31, 32, 35, 39, 51 (bottom), 57 (top), 58, 61, 63, 64, 65 (bottom), 69, 71, 72, 73, 75, 76, 79, 93, 94, 95, 96-7, 98, 99, 103, 106, 107, 108 (right), 110, 112-13, 122, 125, 127, 131, 133, 136 and 137.

Roli Books: Pages 33 and 87.

BIBLIOGRAPHY

Books and articles on Jaipur

Anand, Mulk Raj, (ed.), 1977, *Homage to Jaipur*, Marg, Vol. XXX, no. 4

Asopa, Jai Narayan, (ed.), 1982, *Cultural Heritage of Jaipur*, Jaipur

Bahura, Gopal Narayan, (ed.), 1971, *Catalogue of the Manuscripts in the Maharaja of Jaipur Museum*, Jaipur

-----, 1976, *Literary Heritage of the Rulers of Amber and Jaipur*, Jaipur

-----, (ed.), 1978, *Ramavilasakavyam by Vishwanath Bhatt C. Ranade*, Jaipur

-----, (ed.), 1979, *Sawai Jaisingh Charita by Kavi Atmaram*, Jaipur

-----, (ed.), 1983, *Pratap Prakasa by Krishnadatta Kavi*, Jaipur

Bahura, Gopal Narayan, and Chandramani Singh, 1988, *Catalogue of Historical Documents in Kapad Dwara, Jaipur*, Jaipur

-----, 1990, *Catalogue of Historical Documents in Kapad Dwara, Jaipur: Maps and Plans*, Jaipur

Bailey, Gauvin A., 1995, 'A Portuguese Doctor at the Maharaja of Jaipur's Court', *South Asian Studies*, vol. 11, pp. 51-62

Baylay, C.A., 1879, 'Jaipur', *The Rajputana Gazetteer*, Vol. 2, Calcutta, pp. 125-66

Barker, Sir Robert, 1777, *An Account of the Bramins Observatory at Benares*, London

Benn, R.A.E., 1916, *Notes on Jaipur*, 2nd ed., Jaipur (based on 1st edition, 1909 by H.L. Showers)

Bhatnagar, V.S., 1974, *Life and Times of Sawai Jai Singh 1688-1743*, Delhi

Brooke, J.C., 1868, *Political History of the State of Jaipur*, Selections from the Records of the Government of India, No. XLV, Calcutta

Carapetian, Michael, 1982, 'Jaipur: The Pink City', *The Architectural Review*, vol. CLXXII, no. 1027, pp. 35-43

Crewe, Quentin, 1985, *The Last Maharaja: A Biography of Sawai Man Singh II of Jaipur*, London

Das, A.K., 1985, *The Photographer Prince: Maharaja Sawai Ram Singh II*, City Palace, Jaipur

-----, 1988, 'Maharaja Sawai Ram Singh II: The Photographer Prince', *The India Magazine*, vol. 8, pp. 22-32

Devi, Gayatri, and Santha Rama Rao, 1983, *A Princess Remembers*, 3rd ed., Ghaziabad

Dhama, B.L., 1955, *A Guide to Jaipur and Amber*, 2nd ed., Jaipur

Erdman, Joan L., 1985, *Patrons and Performers in Rajasthan*, Delhi

-----, 1989, 'Jaipur: City Planning in 18th century India', *Shastric Traditions in Indian Arts*, ed. Anna L. Dallapiccola et al., 2 vols, Stuttgart, Vol. 1, pp. 219-35

Garrett, A.ff., and Chandradhar Guleri, 1902, *The Jaipur Observatory and its Builder*, Allahabad

Gode, P.K., 1946, 'Two Contemporary Tributes to Minister Vidyadhara,' *Dr C. Kunha Raja Presentation Volume*, Madras, pp. 285-94

Gole, Susan, 1989, *Indian Maps and Plans: From Earliest Times to the Advent of European Surveys*, New Delhi

Hendley, Thomas Holbein, 1884, *Memorials of the Jeypore Exhibition 1883*, 4 vols, London

-----, 1886, *Jeypore Enamels*, London

-----, 1886, *London Indo-Colonial Exhibition of 1886: Handbook of the Jeypore Courts*, Calcutta

-----, 1892, *Damascening on Steel or Iron, as practised in India*, London

-----, 1895, *A Medico-Topographical Account of Jeypore*, Calcutta

-----, 1896a, *Handbook of the Jeypore Museum*, Delhi

-----, 1896b, *Catalogue of the Collections of the Jeypore Museum*, 2 vols, Delhi

-----, 1905, *Asian Carpets: XVI and XVII Century Designs from the Jaipur Palaces*, 6 parts, London

Hunter, William, 1798, 'Some Account of the Astronomical Labours of Jayasinha, Rajah of Ambhere, or Jayanagar', *Asiatick Researches*, Calcutta, Vol. 5, pp. 177-21

India Office Records, Home Misc. H388, no. 8 (J. Pillet, J. Murray)

Jacob, Sir Samuel Swinton, 1890-1913, *The Jeypore Portfolio of Architectural Details*, 12 vols, London

Jain, Kesharlal Ajmera, and Jawaharlal Jain, (eds), 1935, *The Jaipur Album*, Jaipur

Jaipur Development Authority, 1996, *Jaipur Region Building Bye-Laws*, Jaipur

Kanwar, Dharmendar, 2004, *Rajmata Gayatri Devi … Enduring Grace*, New Delhi

Kaye, G.R., 1918, *The Astronomical Observatories of Jai Singh*, Calcutta

Michell, George, 1978, 'The Plan of Jaipur: A Fusion of Islamic and Indian Ideas', *Storia della Citta*, Vol. 7, pp. 64-8

Nath, Aman, 1993, *Jaipur: The Last Destination*, Bombay

Newell, H.A., 1915, *Jaipur: The Astronomer's City*, London

Nilsson, Sten, 1987, 'Jaipur, In the Sign of Leo', *Magasin Tessin*, no. 1

-----, 1995, 'Jaipur – reflections of a celestial order', *Aspects of Conservation in Urban India*, ed. Sten Nilsson, Lund, pp. 107-128

Pareek, Nand Kishore, 2000, *Jaipur That Was*, Jaipur

Pilania, Gyan Prakash, 2002, *Enlightened Government in Modern India: Heritage of Sawai Jai Singh*, Jaipur

Prakash, Satya, 1955, *Jaipur Brassware in Government Central Museum*, Jaipur

Prakash, Vikramaditya, 1997, 'Identity Production in Postcolonial Indian Architecture', *postcolonial space(s)*, ed. G.B. Nalbantoglu and C.T. Wong, New York, pp. 38-52

Roy, Ashim Kumar, 1978, *History of the Jaipur City*, New Delhi

Rudolph, Susanne Hoeber and Lloyd I., 1984, *Essays on Rajputana*, Delhi

-----, with Mohan Singh Kanota, 2002, *Reversing the Gaze: Amar Singh's Diary, A Colonial Subject's Narrative of Imperial India*, Oxford

Sachdev, Vibhuti, and Giles Tillotson, 2002, *Building Jaipur: The Making of an Indian City*, London

-----, 2008, 'Portraits of the Maharajas of Jaipur', *Portraits of the Princes*, ed. Rosie Llewellyn-Jones, Mumbai

Sahai, Yaduendra, 1981, 'Pink City: its original colour and allied problems', *Cultural Contours of India*, ed. Vijai Shankar Srivastava, New Delhi, pp. 396-400

-----, 1996, *Maharaja Sawai Ram Singh II of Jaipur: The Photographer Prince*, Jaipur

Saksena, Shivnarayan, 1922, *Jaipur Naresh ki England Yatra*, Jaipur

Sarkar, Sir Jadunath, 1984, *A History of Jaipur c. 1503-1938*, ed. Raghubir Sinh, Hyderabad

Sen, Sansar Chander, 1902, *A Short Account of H.H. the Maharajah of Jaipur and his Country*, Ajmer

Sharma, Hanuman, 1919, *Jaipur Naresh Shriman Madhavsinghji*, Calcutta

-----, 1937, *Jaypur Rajya ka Itihas*, repr. Jaipur, 1996

Sharma, M.L., 1969, *History of the Jaipur State*, Jaipur

Sharma, V.N., 1977, *Sawai Jai Singh and His Observatories*, Jaipur

Singh, Chandramani, 1979, *Textiles and Costumes from the Maharaja Sawai Man Singh II Museum*, Jaipur

Singh Kama, Pratap, 1897, *The Lives of their Highness, the Maharaja of Jeypore etc…*, Vizianagram

-----, 1900, *A Brief Sketch of the Life of H.H. the Maharajah of Jaipur*, Vizianagram

Singh, R.P., & Kanwar Rajpal Singh, 2005, *Sawai Man Singh II: Life and Legend*, New Delhi

Somani, G.N., 1922, *Needs and Demands of a Jaipury*, Ajmer

Stern, Robert W., 1988, *The Cat and the Lion: Jaipur State in the British Raj*, Leiden

Stratton, J.P., 1885, *The Jaypur-Amber Family and State*, Jaypur

Tillotson, Giles, 2004, 'The Jaipur Exhibition of 1883', *Journal of the Royal Asiatic Society*, Vol. 14, pt 2, pp. 111-126

-----, 2006, *Jaipur Nama: Tales from the Pink City*, New Delhi

Volwahsen, Andreas, 2001, *Cosmic Architecture: The Astronomical Instruments of Maharaja Jai Singh II*, Prestel, Munich

Jaipur State Reports, State Press Publications etc. (listed chronologically)

Jaipur State Public Works Department (JSPWD), Reports, 1868-1919

Jaipur School of Art, Report, 1878; Illustrated Catalogue, 1897

Jaipur Maharaja's College, Report, 1881

Jaipur Economic and Industrial Museum, Reports, 1882-1898

Jaipur Museum, Acquisition Ledger, 1881-1931

Jaipur Adoption Case, Note by Members of the Mahakma Khas, 1921

Jaipur City Palace, Album of Obituary Notices, 1922

Jaipur State Detailed Budget, 1929

The Jaipur Gazette, 1931

Programme: Birthday Week Celebrations, 1931 & 1932

Programme: The Auspicious Wedding of H.H. the Maharaja Sahib Bahadur with the Princess, Jodhpur, 1932

Programme of the Ceremonies … on the Occasion of the Marriage of Sri Kishor Kanwar Baiji Lal Sahiba, Jodhpur, 1932

Police Arrangements: Fairs, Festivals and State Functions, 1933

Report on the Administration of the Jaipur State, 1935

Jaipur Penal Code, 1935

Memorandum containing the views of the Jaipur State on the Draft Instrument of Accession, 1937

A Glance into the Jaipur Administration, by Raja Gyan Nath, CIE, Prime Minister, Jaipur, 1939

His Highness' Household: Ceremonial Procedure [n.d]

Jaipur War Bulletin, 1941

Working Programme: Wedding of Bai Sahiba Shri Chand Kumari with Raja Bahadur Shri Udai Pratap Singhji of Katiary, 1943

Detailed Working Programme of their Excellencies the Viceroy's and the Viscountess Wavell's Visit to Jaipur, 1946

Speeches by Amin-ul-Mulk Sir Mirza Ismail, KCIE, OBE, Prime Minister of Jaipur, Vol. V, Jaipur, 1947

Jaipur: Issued on the Occasion of the 55th Session of the Indian National Congress, Jaipur, 1948

Beautiful Jaipur, by Henri Cartier-Bresson, Jaipur, 1948

Programme of the Visit of Dr Rajendra Prasad, President of India to Jaipur and Ajmer, 1951

Ceremonial Parade for Unveiling of War Memorial, 1956

A Treasury of Tributes, ed. L.G. Lutter, Jaipur, 1972

General: travel accounts etc.

Battersby, H.F. Prevost, 1906, *India Under Royal Eyes*, London

Beaton, Cecil, 1945, *Indian Album*, London

Boileau, A.H.E., 1837, *Personal Narrative of a Tour through the Western States of Rajwarra, in 1835*, Calcutta

Diver, Maud, 1942, *Royal India*, London

Fayrer, Sir J., 1879, *Notes of the Visits to India of Their Royal Highnesses the Prince of Wales and the Duke of Edinburgh*, London

Forbes, Rosita, 1939, *India of the Princes*, London

Francklin, William, 1798, *The History of the Reign of Shah-Aulum*, London

Heber, Reginald, 1828, *Narrative of a Journey through the Upper Provinces of India from Calcutta to Bombay*, 3 vols, London

Hendley, Thomas Holbein, 1897, *The Rulers of India and the Chiefs of Rajputana*, London

Huxley, Aldous, 1926, *Jesting Pilate: The Diary of a Journey*, London

Ismail, Sir Mirza, 1954, *My Public Life*, London

Jacquemont, Victor, 1834, *Letters from India*, 2 vols, London

-----, 1841, *Voyage dans l'Inde*, 4 vols, Paris

Journal of Indian Art, Vols 1-3, 1886-90, London

Kipling, Rudyard, 1907, *From Sea to Sea: Letters of Travel*, 2 vols, New York

Reed, Stanley, 1906, *The Royal Tour in India*, Bombay

Rousselet, Louis, 1876, *India and its Native Princes*, ed. Lt. Col. Buckle, London

Sanderson, Gordon, 1913, *Types of Modern Indian Buildings*, Allahabad

Sharma, Ram Shankar, 1909, *Paribhraman athva Shrinathrajyabhishek Darshan*, Bankipur

Tieffenthaler, Joseph, 1786, 'La Geographie de l'Indoustan', transl. (from Latin) Jean Bernoulli, *Description Historique et Geographique de l'Inde*, 3 vols, Berlin, vol. 1

Tod, Lt. Col. James, 1972, *Annals and Antiquities of Rajasthan*, 2 vols, (1829/32), repr. London

Waddington, C.W., 1933, *Indian India as Seen by a Guest in Rajasthan*, London

Other general works consulted

Acharya, P.K. (transl.), 1934, *Architecture of Manasara*, repr. New Delhi, 1980

Bayly, C.A., (ed.), 1990, *The Raj: India and the British, 1600-1947*, NPG, London

Bhandari, M.M. 1978, *Flora of the Indian Desert*, Jodhpur

Case, Margaret H., (ed.), 1986, *Govindadeva: A Dialogue in Stone*, IGNCA, New Delhi

Chakrabarti, Vibhuti [Sachdev], 1998, *Indian Architectural Theory*, London (and OUP Delhi, 1999)

Chundawat, Rani Lakshmi Kumari, 1994, *Sanskritik Rajasthan*, Jaipur

Dagens, Bruno, (transl.), 1985, *Mayamata: An Indian Treatise on Housing, Architecture and Iconography*, New Delhi

Falconer, John, 2001, *India: Pioneering Photographers, 1850-1900*, London

Hooja, Rima, 2007, *A History of Rajasthan*, New Delhi

Johnson, Robert Flynn, ed., 2004, *Reverie and Reality: Nineteenth-Century Photographs of India from the Ehrenfeld Collection*, San Francisco

Moynihan, Elizabeth, 1982, *Paradise as a Garden in Persia and Mughal India*, London

National Gallery of Modern Art, 1995, *A Shifting Focus: Photography in India 1850-1900*, New Delhi

Pelizzari, Maria Antonella, ed., 2003, *Traces of India: Photography, Architecture, and the Politics of Representation, 1850-1900*, Montreal & New Haven

Pinney, Christopher, 1997, *Camera Indica: The Social Life of Indian Photographs*, London

Sarkar, B.K., transl., 1975, *The Sukraniti* (1st ed. 1914), repr. New Delhi

Tillotson, G.H.R., 1987, *The Rajput Palaces*, New Haven & London/ OUP Delhi

-----, 1989, *The Tradition of Indian Architecture*, New Haven & London/ OUP Delhi

-----, (ed.), 2001, *Stones in the Sand: The Architecture of Rajasthan*, Mumbai

Vinnels, David, and Brent Skelly, 2002, *Bollywood Showplaces: Cinema Theatres in India*, London

Worswick, Clark, 1980, *Princely India: Photographs by Raja Deen Dayal 1884-1910*, London

INDEX